The Essence of Small Business

2nd Edition

THE ESSENCE OF MANAGEMENT SERIES

Published Titles

The Essence of Total Quality Management
The Essence of Small Business
The Essence of Consumer Behaviour
The Essence of Strategic Management
The Essence of International Money (2nd edition)
The Essence of Financial Accounting (2nd edition)
The Essence of Management Accounting (2nd edition)
The Essence of Marketing Research
The Essence of Change
The Essence of Personnel Management and Industrial Relations
The Essence of Information Systems (2nd edition)
The Essence of Competitive Strategy
The Essence of Statistics for Business (2nd edition)
The Essence of Operations Management
The Essence of Negotiation
The Essence of Effective Communication
The Essence of Marketing
The Essence of Human Resource Management
The Essence of Financial Management
The Essence of Business Economics (2nd edition)
The Essence of the Economy (2nd edition)
The Essence of International Marketing
The Essence of Services Marketing
The Essence of Business Process Re-engineering
The Essence of Business Ethics
The Essence of Management Creativity
The Essence of Mathematics for Business
The Essence of Mergers and Acquisitions
The Essence of International Business
The Essence of Organizational Behaviour
The Essence of Women in Management
The Essence of Managing Groups and Teams
The Essence of Managing People

The Essence of Small Business

2nd Edition

COLIN BARROW

Prentice Hall Europe

London New York Toronto Sydney Tokyo Singapore
Madrid Mexico City Munich Paris

First published 1993
This edition published 1998 by
Prentice Hall Europe
Campus 400, Maylands Avenue
Hemel Hempstead
Hertfordshire, HP2 7EZ
A division of
Simon & Schuster International Group

Typeset in 10/12pt Palatino by Hands Fotoset, Ratby, Leicestershire

Printed and bound in Great Britain by
T. J. International Ltd.

Library of Congress Cataloging-in-Publication Data

Barrow, Colin.
The essence of small business / Colin Barrow. — 2nd ed.
p. cm. — (The Essence of management series)
Includes bibliographical references and index.
ISBN 0-13-748641-3 (alk. paper).
1. Small business. 2. Small business—Management. I. Title.
II. Series.
HD2341.B273 1998
658.02'2—dc21 97–38534
CIP

British Library Cataloguing in Publication Data

A catalogue record for this book is available from
the British Library

ISBN 0-13-748641-3

1 2 3 4 5 02 01 00 99 98

Contents

Preface

The number of people running their own business, despite the recessions of the 1980s and early 1990s, is still considerable. In the United Kingdom alone the small business population has grown from around 2 million in 1980 to more than 3.5 million in 1997. Across Europe one worker in eight runs their own business, and in Japan and the United States the figures are higher still. But to launch a small business or expand an existing one successfully is not a simple task. Good ideas, hard work, enthusiasm, skills and knowledge about your product and how to make it, though essential, are not enough. Evidence for this is the substantial volume of business failures and liquidations. By the mid-1990s company failures across Europe alone exceeded 200,000 a year, nearly double the figure for the start of the decade. To be sure, the adverse economic situation was responsible for some of those failures. But even in the relatively buoyant late 1990s, over 300,000 business of all types 'die' each year in the United Kingdom alone. Most of these failures occur within the first few years. These facts have made it increasingly clear that small businesses need special help, particularly in their formative period. For example, owners and managers often need help in acquiring business skills in such areas as basic book-keeping and accounting. Most failing businesses simply do not know their financial position. The order book is very often full when the cash runs out. Then they need information with which to make realistic market assessments of the size and possibilities of their chosen market. Overoptimism about the size and ease with which a market can be reached is an all too common mistake.

Owners and managers also need to know what sorts of finance are available and how to put themselves in the best possible position to raise it. Surprisingly, there is no shortage of funds. Problems lie, rather, in the business proposition itself, or, more often, in the way in which the proposition is made to the financier. This calls for a 'business plan', a statement of business purpose, with the consequences spelt out in financial terms. For example, you must describe what you want your business to do, who its customers will be, how much they will spend, who will supply you, how much their supplies will cost. Then you must translate those plans and projections into cash: how much your business will need, how much you already have, how much you expect 'outsiders' to put in. For most people this calls for new knowledge. They have never prepared a business plan before, and they do not know how to start.

This plan will also help them to escape the 'pneumonia' of small businesses – underestimation of the amount of start-up capital they will need. It is difficult, if not impossible, to go back to a bank and ask for another 30% of funding six months after opening the doors, and retain any credibility at all. And yet this is what happens. New businesses consistently underestimate how much they will need to finance growth. Most end up struggling where they need not have struggled, or failing where there was no 'market' reason for failure.

Inventors and technologists have special problems of communication and security when they try to translate their ideas into businesses. All too often their inventions have been left for other countries to exploit, or else they feel unhappy about discussing ideas, believing that a patent is their only protection. But more often than not they simply do not know who to talk to, little realizing that sophisticated help is often close at hand. Thus a path from the laboratory to the marketplace has to be illuminated so that small firms and inventors can see a clear route. New technologies have to be made available to new business. The microcomputer, which has revolutionized big business, has now begun to knock on the doors of smaller businesses. For this reason these firms have to know how to exploit this technology and so remain competitive – or they may join the ranks of the failures.

New and revived business opportunities are springing up to meet the needs and aspirations of would-be 'entrepreneurs'. Franchising, workers' cooperatives and management buy-outs are just three such areas. These have grown from relative obscurity in the late 1980s to being major business opportunities in the 1990s.

This book is aimed at those who either want to review their prospects in the small business world, or who want as part of a wider study to gain an appreciation of the issues that surround the small business founder – their motivations, aspirations, problems and opportunities. It brings together, from a wide variety of sources, the essential elements of knowledge that are a prerequisite to understanding the world of small business.

Colin Barrow
May 1997

1

Small business today

Recent years have seen a major resurgence of small business throughout the developed world which even the recessions of the 1980s and 1990s have done little to abate. In eastern Europe and the Soviet Union, throughout Asia and now in China, such skills are greatly prized.

In most developed economies anything from 6% to 15% of the working population are small-business men and women. This, for example, translates into about 3.4 million people in the United Kingdom, out of a working population of around 27 million. Over half of all the people in commercial and industrial employment in the United Kingdom work in a small business.

In Italy 90% of all industrial firms are small businesses and absorb 84% of total employment. In Denmark 92% of all manufacturing firms are small businesses employing 43% of the workforce.

But throughout history small business has received only modest attention. Few historians have bothered to record its contributions to society, even though the first known piece of writing appeared more than 4,000 years ago. It described how bankers loaned money at interest.[1] Since then, small-business people have been the innovative backbone of most economies, providing products and services to benefit the consumer.

Small business flourished in almost all ancient cultures. The Arab, Babylonian, Egyptian, Jewish, Greek, Phoenician and Roman populations contained a substantial number of small businesses. Their products and services, however, were often of poor quality. Consumers were often cheated and defrauded. The result was that small businesses became objects of contempt.

To protect consumers from unscrupulous small business proprietors, Hammurabi, King of Babylon, drafted a code of 300 laws. Carved on marble columns 8 feet high, the original code now resides at the Louvre Museum in Paris, though much of it has been erased by time. Two of Hammurabi's laws follow:

> If outlaws hatch a conspiracy in the house of a wineseller and she does not arrest them and bring them to the palace, that wineseller shall be put to death.
>
> If a builder has built a house for a man and does not make his work perfect; and the house which he has built has fallen down and so caused the death of the householders, that builder shall be put to death.[2]

So even 4,000 years ago it was considered necessary to protect consumers from business and business from the consumers. It is also interesting to note that the first law deals with business women and their social responsibilities towards government.

Despite many successes, small-business history, until recent years, has never excited the public at large. Greek and Roman historians virtually ignored small business. In their view, ideas and military deeds were the stuff of history. Yet it was largely through small business that civilization was spread throughout the known world. Small businesses transported such things as Babylonian astronomy and Greek philosophy, the Jewish calendar and Roman law.

In the centuries that followed, most religions held small-business people in low esteem. The Church branded retailers as sinners because they did nothing to improve a product, but charged a higher price. And, until the nineteenth century, the Church often spoke against the practice of charging interest on loans.

Although now held in higher esteem than ever before, small business remains overshadowed by professions such as medicine and law. As one business historian points out:

> Physicians are now wrapped in such dignity that the public forgets how recently they occupied the status of barbers. Lawyers have climbed from the solicitor–family relation to a solemn eminence. Not so the businessman; he still struggles on, unfathered and unhallowed. He is his own ancestor, and usually, his memory does not reach back even to the last business crisis.[3]

Definitions of small business, using size

Small business defies easy definition. Typically, we apply the term 'small business' to so-called one-man bands such as neighbourhood shops and restaurants, and we apply the term 'big business' to such giants as IBM, General Motors, Shell and ICI. But between these two extremes fall businesses that may be looked upon as big or small, depending on the yard-stick and cut-off point used to measure size.

The Small Business Administration (SBA), founded by the US government in 1953 for the purpose of providing intermediate to long-term financing for small businesses that could not obtain money on reasonable terms elsewhere, has a definition of a small business which embraces almost 99% of full-time businesses (see Table 1.1).

The SBA goes to great lengths by even defining smallness differently by industry sector, within each main business category (see Table 1.2).

Those definitions are by no means hard and fast, and they can be relaxed in exceptional cases. In 1966, for example, the SBA classified American Motors as small to enable the company to bid on certain government contracts. At the time, American Motors ranked as the nation's sixty-third largest manufacturer, with 32,000 employees and sales revenue of $991 million. The SBA justified its judgement by applying a seldom-used test of smallness – namely, that a business qualifies as small if it does not dominate its industry. American Motors easily met that test.

Table 1.1 Small US business as defined by the SBA

Category	Sales ($ million)	Employment
Retail	2–8	
Wholesale	9.5–22	
Construction	1.0–9.5	
Manufacturing		0–1,500
Agriculture	1.0	

Table 1.2 SBA standards of smallness for selected industries

Manufacturers	**Employing fewer than**
Aircraft	1,500 persons
Calculating machines	1,000
Household vacuum cleaners	750
Men's and boys' clothes	500
Macaroni and spaghetti	250
Retailers	**Earning sales of less than**
Mail order houses	$7.5 million a year
Grocery stores	7.5
Automobile agencies	6.5
Variety stores	3.0
Radio and television stores	2.5
Wholesalers	**Earning sales of less than**
Paints and varnishes	$22.0 million a year
Tyres and tubes	22.0
Groceries	14.5
Sporting goods	14.5

Source: 'SBA rules and regulations', *The Code of Federal Regulation*, (Washington, DC: US Government Printing Office, 5 October 1978), section 121, 3–10.

Many of the SBA's definitions really cover medium-sized businesses. For example, a manufacturer employing 1,000 people probably has sales revenue in excess of $50 million a year. Few people would really view such a business as small.

In the United Kingdom a committee was set up in July 1969 under the chairmanship of J. E. Bolton[4] to consider the state of small firms in the national economy and the facilities available to them, and to make recommendations.

Small firms were at that stage defined as those with less than 200 employees. The committee found this definition somewhat unhelpful and added some views of its own. It felt that the firm should have a relatively small share of its market, it should be run by its owner and should be independent and not the subsidiary of a larger firm. The quantitative limits were set at 200 employees in manufacturing firms, an annual turnover of £50,000 per annum (1970 prices) in retailing and 25 employees in construction.

Two other studies in the United Kingdom, under the chairmanship of Sir Harold Wilson[5] and Harold Macmillan,[6] saw small firms as differing from large firms mainly in the way in which they were financed. For example, the small firm is more reliant on bank finance and the use of trade creditors. Small, and for that matter medium-sized, firms were characterized by their inability to raise risk capital from the public, depending instead on the owner's stake and loans from directors.

In France the usual translation of 'small business' yields the phrase *petite et moyenne entreprise* (small and medium-sized enterprise), abbreviated as PME. However, this term excludes those companies with less than ten employees, representing over 90% of all businesses and employing about one-sixth of the total workforce. These very small businesses predominate in *artisanat* (crafts), non-food retailing, the hotel and restaurant trade and automobile repairs and distribution.

In France, as in most countries, there is no single official definition of 'small business'. However, numerous quantitative definitions are used in taxation, industrial relations and government incentives. The most widely used (and widely criticized) definition is based on employment:

- ☐ Less than 10 employees: *artisanat* and very small enterprises.
- ☐ 10 to 40 employees: small enterprises.
- ☐ 50 to 500 employees: medium-sized enterprises.
- ☐ Over 500 employees: large enterprises.

It should be noted that the term 'employees' only includes salaried employment and thus generally excludes the owner-manager and their immediate family members. Over half of the businesses in France have no salaried employees.

In France the threshold of fifty employees has long been important, since this is the level at which a works committee becomes obligatory. Many owner-managers, concerned that this committee could limit their authority and independence, are known to have created new businesses in parallel rather than cross this threshold. The lowering of the thresholds in recent years has altered the significance of the 50-employee barrier. The term PMI (*petites et moyennes entreprises industrielles*) covers those PMEs engaged in industrial activities – this does not include building and civil works. Below ten employees, a distinction is drawn between the *artisanat* and other very small businesses.

Certain financial incentives are available to individuals and companies registered with the Chambres des Métiers (Craft Chambers), registration being restricted to businesses with less than ten employees (not counting certain family members and apprentices) and carrying on specified crafts.

These crafts essentially require the direct involvement of the owner of the business in the production, and include such activities as baking, butchery, plumbing, building and carpentry. The owner may also be a qualified craftsperson or master craftsperson, but this is not required for registration.

Turnover figures are principally used for fiscal purposes. If sales are below 1.8 million French francs (FFr), certain simplified income tax returns may be applicable.

Smaller countries such as Denmark and Eire have definitions that more appropriately narrow their size. In Denmark, for example, a small business is one with under 49 employees, a medium one has 50–199 employees and a large business employs over 200 people. Denmark only has 400 firms that meet the large business (LB) definition; if it adopted the American definition it would have virtually no large businesses. Inevitably the EU has its own definition, the latest version of which emerged in 1996. To be small a firm must employ between 10 and 49 people or turnover more than £5.6 million or have more than £4 million in the balance sheet. Anything smaller is micro and greater is medium. With over 500 employees, a firm is considered large. Figure 1.1 and Table 1.3, though only covering the United Kingdom and the United States, give a good example of business in developed countries.

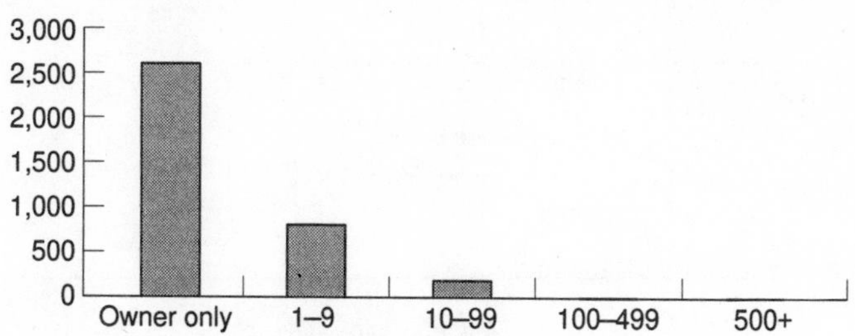

Figure 1.1 Number of UK firms by number of employees (source DTI statistics, 1995).

Table 1.3 Percentage of small business in the United States

Percentage of businesses	Number of employees fewer than
88.9%	10 persons
94.7	20
99.2	100
99.9	500

Source: US Department of Commerce, *Enterprise Statistics*, 1990.

Organizational definitions of small business

A more helpful definition of a small business is a firm that is small relative to its market, managed by its owners, and not part of a large enterprise.

The American organization researcher, L. E. Greiner,[7] identified five distinctive phases in a company's growth pattern, and provided an insight into the changes in organizational structure, strategy and behaviour that need to be achieved if it is to move on to the next phase and so become a larger business (see Figure 1.2). By implication his research revealed that most firms never learn the lessons, or at any rate not in time. At best they bounce up and down against the frontiers of the phase they are in. At worst they fail and flounder.

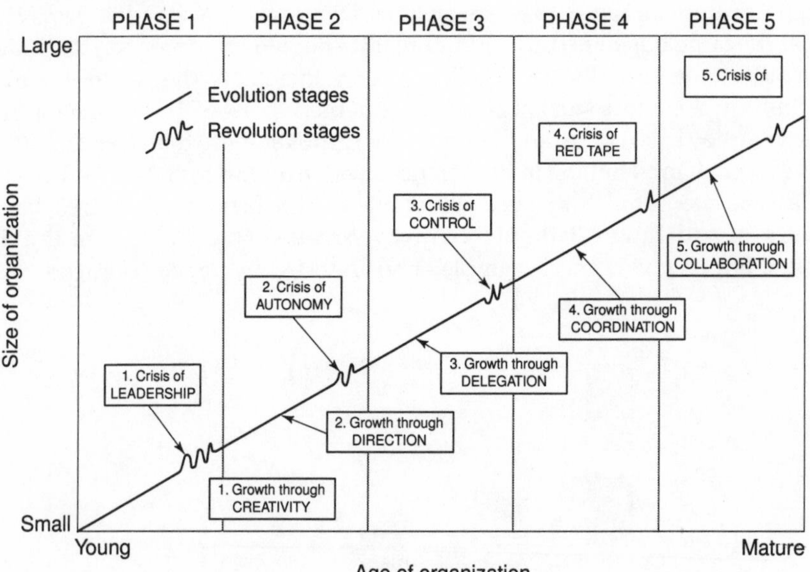

Figure 1.2 Organizational phases of growth: the five phases of growth (source: L. E. Greiner, *Harvard Business Review*, July/August 1972).

Phase 1: growth through creativity

Any business starting up does so because somebody has a good idea about providing a product or service for which they believe there is good demand. If the idea is successful, then the business can grow or evolve with equal success. The founder of the company is at the heart of everything. Assuming that the business has been successful and shows steady growth – a description that fits only between 60% and 70% of start-ups as the rest have already failed by this stage – there comes a time when the person who started the business with their creative ideas and personal, informal style of operation can no longer cope effectively. The person who provided all the drive, all the ideas and made all the decisions becomes overloaded with administrative detail and operational problems. Unless the founder can change the organizational structure of their firm and put in place a management team, any further growth will leave the business as vulnerable as it was before. It will be incapable of becoming a substantial firm with a life independent from that of its founder. A cycle of one step forward and two steps back will probably begin, or else a gentle decline will set in. The end of this first growth phase, which can take anything from a few years to decades in extreme cases, is signalled by a 'crisis' of leadership.

Table 1.4 provides some idea of exactly how dangerous this opportunity is, as over 50% of businesses that fail do so in less than five years – a further 25% go in less than ten years.To some extent this improved capacity for survival can be explained by the experience gained by owner-managers in dealing with the problems they encounter. Over time, as researcher Graham Hall[8] has shown, a small firm will meet increasingly less fresh problems and will be able to draw on experience to meet successive threats. The longer the period that elapses, the less the likelihood that such threats have not been successfully confronted before; hence the longer its track record, the longer a firm is likely to stay in business in the future. Barriers to entry will also play a part in causing a firm to fail early in its life. Low barriers to entry lead to fast overcrowding within a market. But business opportunities requiring few resources or skills are, by definition, attractive to many people. Dunne *et al.*,[9] who researched this topic, found a correlation between an above average volume of start-ups in a sector and an above average failure rate in the following period.

Phase 2: growth through direction

A strong leader is required to pull the company through this crisis. They must be able to make tough decisions about priorities and provide clear,

Table 1.4 Ages of 61,209 businesses in the UK that failed in 1987

Age of business	All types combined %	Manufacturing %	Wholesale trade %	Retail trade %	Services %
1 year or less	10.0	7.8	7.7	12.0	14.9
2 years	12.4	13.0	12.5	15.9	12.7
3 years	11.4	11.3	11.3	13.7	11.2
4 years	9.4	9.9	9.5	10.1	8.9
5 years	7.5	7.0	8.4	7.6	7.8
Total 5 years or less	50.7	49.0	49.4	59.3	55.5
6–10 years	24.6	23.3	25.5	22.0	24.6
Over 10 years	24.7	27.7	25.1	18.7	19.9
Total	100.0	100.0	100.0	100.0	100.0

Source: Dunn and Bradstreet, *Business Failures, 1987*, 1988.

single-minded direction and the sense of purpose needed to move the business forward.

Ideas that the pioneer founder used to carry in their head now have to be formalized. Policies need to be evolved, teams built up and key people appointed with specific roles to play and objectives to achieve. The personal management style of the founder becomes secondary to making the business efficient. Sometimes the founder is no longer the right person to lead the organization through this phase and, either through lack of management skills or temperament, they may opt to give up or sell out.

Success at this stage of growth depends on finding, motivating and keeping key staff – no mean task. A Cranfield Study[10] concluded that over 80% of the proprietors of growing firms rated this a major problem, compared with around 50% who were most concerned about finding customers and only 25% who rated raising money or high interest rates as a top issue.

Eventually, as the company grows and matures, the directive 'top-down' management style starts to become counterproductive. Others working in the organization acquire more expertise in their particular sphere of operations than the central 'director'; not surprisingly, they want a greater say in the strategy of the business. Such subordinates either struggle for power so that they can be heard, or become demotivated and leave. This is the crisis autonomy and, if it is not recognized and managed, it will absorb so much energy and time that it will drag the company down. In the same study referred to earlier, three out of five of the growth companies surveyed reported the loss of key employees. Two-thirds of them experienced this loss within a year of making the appointment.

Proprietors usually give the reason for the loss of key employees as 'better pay elsewhere'. In this they are usually wrong. A MORI poll conducted in 1989 for the Industrial Society on 1,000 employees asked people to identify the five most important things they looked for in a job: 66% said having an interesting and enjoyable job; 52% said job security; 41% said feeling that they had accomplished something worthwhile; 37% said basic pay; and 30% regarded the chance to learn new skills as being of prime importance.

Interestingly enough, this study concluded that employers generally saw pay as the key factor in recruiting and retaining staff, and only 11% thought job satisfaction was an important factor.

Phase 3: growth through delegation

The solution to the crisis of autonomy is to recognize that more responsibility has to be delegated to more people in the company. The trouble is that most founders hang on to too many jobs in their firms, mostly out of a belief that nobody else can do the job as well as them. The reasons for this argument are legion:

- ☐ It takes more time to explain the job than to do it myself.
- ☐ A mistake would be too costly.
- ☐ They lack the experience – and so on.

There is probably an element of truth in all of these reasons, but until you learn how to delegate decisions rather than simply to dump tasks, your organization will never reach full maturity.

Two problems arise at this stage. First, a number of the 'managers' appointed earlier on will simply not be up to the task of accepting the new responsibilities. Not all people who can take direction can take part in a 'bottom-up' planning process that is dependent on high quality inputs. So this means that founders are back in the recruiting game. They could be wise at this stage to stop relying on personal contacts or direct-press advertising as the majority of small firms do, and go for executive search through a consultancy using sound selection techniques. They probably thought this too expensive at Phase I and possibly so at Phase II – but by now founders will have made enough mistakes in recruitment to know that it is a profession in its own right and requires the knowledge and skill that they may not have. Furthermore, the indirect costs of getting the wrong people more than outweigh the cost of paying for an expert.

One owner-manager was a little startled, to say the least, when he discovered that doing the recruitment himself cost him over six times as much as using an agency. Table 1.5 shows the differences in business structure, systems and styles/people, and the relative strengths and weaknesses at each stage in a small firm's growth.

The second point to be aware of is that every solution creates new problems. For example, delegating decisions to give people a strong sense of involvement will eventually lead to control problems.

Table 1.5 The stages of growth

	Phase I Creativity	Phase 2 Direction	Phase 3 Delegation	Phase 4 Coordination	Phase 5 Collaboration
Structure	Informal	Functional Centralized Hierarchical Top-down	Decentralized Bottom-up	Staff functions Introduced SBUs Decentralized Units merged into product groups	Matrix-type structure
Systems	Immediate response to customer feedback	Standards Cost centres Budget Salary systems	Profit centres Bonuses Management by exception	Formal planning procedures Investment centres Tight expenditure controls	Simplified and integrated information systems
Styles/people	Individualistic Creative Entrepreneurial ownership	Strongly directive Impersonal	Full delegation and autonomy	Watchdog	Team-oriented Inter-personal Skills at a premium Innovative Educational bias
Strengths	Fun Market response	Efficient	High management motivation	More efficient allocation of corporate and local resources	Greater spontaneity Flexible and behavioural approach
Crisis point	Crisis of leadership	Crisis of autonomy	Crisis of control	Crisis of red tape	?
Weaknesses	Founder often temperament-ally unsuited to managing Boss overloaded	Unsuited diversity Cumbersome hierarchy Doesn't grow People	Top managers lose control as freedom breeds parochial attitudes	Bureaucratic divisions between line/staff, headquarters/ field, etc.	Psychological saturation

Finally, it is as well to remember that evolution and growth in business are not automatic. It is the chief executive's job to know when the time for strategic change has come and exactly what that strategy should be.

But even with good management teams in place, further problems can occur. Once managers to whom one can delegate are in operation, they will make their own decisions, as well as the decisions delegated to them. In time, the organization will become increasingly fragmented and uncoordinated. This often becomes apparent in fairly dramatic ways, such as loss of profits, margin erosion, unplanned development and the lack of an overall strategy to which everyone can be committed. Another crisis looms: the crisis of control.

Phase 4: growth through coordination

During this phase the crisis of control is overcome by achieving the best of both the delegation and the direction phases. Decision-making (and power) is still delegated, but in a systematic and regulated way. Accountability becomes a byword for the first time. At this point the organization begins to put in place strategic planning of some sort, to combine bottom-up and top-down planning methods. Systems and policies are developed to regulate the behaviour of managers at all levels. Communication is vital and a corporate culture takes shape, giving 'new people' a feel for the way that things are done in the company.

This growth phase usually ends in the crisis of red tape, where the clutter of rules and regulations that bind it results in missed opportunities. Bureaucracy rules, and development and initiative are stifled. This crisis can be overcome, or even circumvented, by introducing innovative, non-bureaucratic planning procedures, or by subdividing the business into management units with their own separate missions and management. This is fine as long as founders do not return these units back to a Phase 1-type growth in a desperate bid to release creativity.

Phase 5: growth through collaboration

The way to circumvent red tape is to inculcate an attitude of collaboration throughout the organization. This calls for simplified and integrated information systems and an emphasis on team-oriented activity.

Many successful Japanese and European firms now organize their workforces into teams, where there used to be production lines. Volvo, for example, has a team responsible for making and assembling the whole of one car. This has the effect of making a group of people responsible for the whole of one major portion of a task, rather than having individuals responsible for small and sometimes rather meaningless parts of the process. In this way people can be encouraged to generate solutions rather than just pass problems on down the line.

A further emphasis at this stage of growth is on management education and personal development. This activity is viewed as a luxury in a new venture, and as a good investment in a mature venture.

Most small businesses will lie somewhere between crisis of leadership and the fourth stage of growth, using Greiner's model. It is useful for founders to keep some points in mind as they steer a course through these troubled and largely uncharted waters.

First, tempting though it will be, do not try to skip phases out of impatience. Each phase results in certain strengths and learning experiences which are essential for success in subsequent phases. When one owner-manager was introduced to this way of looking at growth, the scales fell from his eyes. He had tried to delegate authority and involve his key managers in developing strategy almost from the time he launched the business. There was not a clear enough set of goals for them to aim for, and one after another they left. The organization nearly failed too. This was as a direct result of trying to move too quickly from Phase 1 to Phase 3, skipping Phase 2.

Some other definitions that are important in the small-business world include the following.

Entrepreneurs

An entrepreneur is someone who recognizes an opportunity, raises the money and other resources needed to exploit that opportunity, and takes some or all of the risk associated with executing the ensuing plans.

Entrepreneurship can be more correctly viewed as a behaviour characteristic than a personal trait, which explains why the 'typical' entrepreneur is difficult to describe – or to detect in advance using questionnaires. One author, after interviewing 400 successful entrepreneurs, came up with this thumbnail sketch of the characteristics of successful entrepreneurs:

- 27–33 years old.
- Heterosexual male (95%).
- Simple hairstyle and frequently bearded.
- Wear casual comfortable clothes and no jewellery.
- Enjoy excellent health, no excesses such as smoking or drinking.
- Sixty-five per cent divorced, 35% still with first wife, no bachelors.
- Live in urban areas (majority).
- Middle-class backgrounds and good communication skills (majority).
- Drive a European car of the largely maintenance-free variety (80%).
- Vote Labour/SDP (80%).

However, it would not be that difficult to come up with 400 others who do not fit this picture at all. Most people equate entrepreneurship with either new or small businesses. The literal translation they rely on is that of the 'owner-manager', a term used to distinguish the 'boss' who also owns the business from the professionals who are hired to run it. This rather narrow appreciation is misleading and mistakenly excludes the big established ventures, including those owned by governments, from having a need for entrepreneurs.

The term 'entrepreneur' was introduced into economics by Cantillon (1755) and raised to prominence by the French economist J. B. Say around 1800. He used it to describe someone who 'shifts economic resources out of an area of lower and into an area of higher productivity and greater yield'. (Say was an admirer of Adam Smith and translated his *Wealth of Nations* into French.)

Classical economics, with its focus on getting the most out of existing resources, does not provide an adequate vehicle for handling the entrepreneur. Indeed, most classical economists and the modern schools (from Keynesians to Friedmanites) consign the entrepreneur to the ethereal realm of 'external forces' along with the weather, governments, pestilence and war.

Although some economists recognize their existence, they simply do not accommodate entrepreneurs in their models of the economy. (You can test this for yourself by reading the index of any ten major economics textbooks. Seven will have no entry at all under the heading 'entrepreneur'; one will devote a paragraph to justify their exclusion; and the remainder will devote not more than a page to the subject.)

Joseph Schumpeter was the first major modern economist to return to Say's ideas. In the *Theory of Economic Dynamics* (1911) he postulated that dynamic disequilibrium induced by the innovating entrepreneur, rather than optimization and the balancing of needs and resources, is the norm in a healthy economy.

By this definition, most new business start-ups are not truly entrepreneurial and many are simply poor copies of existing businesses, in that they are not shifting economic resources to an area of higher productivity and greater yield. (At best they are moving sideways and at worst down and out.)

Intrapreneurs

The term was coined in the United States in 1979 by Giffard Pinchot III to describe the process whereby big companies set out to encourage entrepreneurial characteristics in their own managers. In other words, if people come to work with good ideas, stop them going home with them.

One classic example is Art Fry of 3M, who intrapreneured the Post-It notepads – those little yellow stickers that embellish so many sheets of company notepaper and business reports. Fry had an unshakeable conviction that these stickers could be produced and marketed successfully by 3M, although the product itself ran contrary to the corporate culture (their business was making things stick together, not pull apart!). But he also knew that the resistance and inertia typical in most big firms could kill the product at birth. Fry used the 3M senior management encouragement and entrepreneurial skill to move the product forward quickly with the minimum resources and so created a resoundingly successful and profitable product.

The Swedish group, Forsight, founded the first school for intrapreneurs, where programmes tailored to client companies teach employees how to develop their ideas and teach top management how to deal with them.

Corporate ventures

Pioneered in the late 1960s in the United States by 3M and Dupont, corporate venturing is the process by which mature and usually big businesses look outside the company for new ideas. Underlying most of this activity is a desire to get early access to new technologies and at the same time to freshen up their own organization's entrepreneurial verve.

Typically, the corporate venturer seeks to invest in a spread of new small businesses through venture capital funds, and so set up an early warning system for technological developments. For example, Monsanto, the US chemicals group, has put some $50 million into nine funds around the world, mostly managed by the British Venture Capital Association. An alternative, adopted by Ferranti, is to launch an internally managed venture capital fund and so invest money and management expertise directly into new ventures.

References

1. Bursk, Edward C., *The World of Business* (New York: Macmillan, 1963), 1, 2.
2. Driver, G. R. and Miles, John C., *The Babylonian Laws* (Oxford: Clarendon Press, 1955), II, 83.
3. Beard, Miriam, *A History of the Business Man* (New York: Macmillan, 1938), 1, 1.
4. The Bolton Report (Cmnd 4811, 1971).
5. The Wilson Committee (Cmnd 7937, 1979).
6. The Macmillan Committee (Cmnd 3897, 1931).
7. Greiner, L. E., 'Evolution and revolution as organisations grow', *Harvard Business Review*, July/August 1972.
8. Hall, Graham, *Surviving and Prospering in the Small Firms Sector* (London: Routledge, 1995).
9. Dunne, T., Roberts, M. J. and Samuelson, L., 'Patterns of firm entry and exit in US manufacturing industries', *Rand Journal of Economics*, **19**, 4 (1988), pp. 495–515.
10. Key Staff Employment Study, Cranfield School of Management, 1990.

2

The small-business person

Why they matter and why they often fail

The characteristics of a small-business person

To launch a new business successfully calls for a particular type of person. The business idea must also be right for the market and the timing must be spot on. The world of business failures is full of products that are ahead of their time.

The business founder is frequently seen as someone who is always bursting with new ideas, is highly enthusiastic, hyperactive and insatiably curious. But the more you try to create a picture of the typical small-business founder, the more elusive they become.

Peter Drucker, the international business guru, captured the problem clearly with this description:

> Some are eccentrics, others painfully correct conformists; some are fat and some are lean; some are worriers, some relaxed; some drink quite heavily, others are total abstainers; some are men of great charm and warmth, some have no more personality than a frozen mackerel.

Many such efforts have been made to 'define' the characteristics of those people who are best suited to become small-business proprietors. These efforts will no doubt continue, but it is unlikely that they will be any more successful than production techniques are today.

The following fairly broad characteristics are generally accepted as being 'essential', but such evidence as there is to support this view is largely anecdotal.

Total commitment and hard work

Small-business founders have complete faith in their business idea. That is the only way that they can convince all the doubters that they are bound to meet on the way. They are usually single-minded and more than capable of putting in an eighteen-hour working day. This can put a strain on other relationships, so successful small-business founders usually involve their families and get them on their side too.

Small-business proprietors are also likely to put in many more hours at work than their employees. This is true for both male and female small-business people, although generally male proprietors do seem to work longer hours than their female equivalent.

In the United Kingdom at any rate, over the decade of the 1980s the proportion of small-business people working more than forty-one hours per week increased (see Table 2.1). For male business founders this increase was more noticeable. (This is probably because many female business founders have part-time ventures.)

Until recently it has been the workaholic who has epitomized the spirit of enterprise, and according to research by Professor Gary Cooper, a

Table 2.1 Self-employed and employees by hours worked

	1981		1989	
	Employee	Self-employed	Employee	Self-employed
All				
0–12	6	5	7	7
13–32	16	9	16	12
33–40	62	29	36	20
41–56	13	29	34	34
57+	3	29	6	27
Total	100	100	100	100
Male				
0–12	1	2	2	3
13–32	4	4	3	6
33–40	71	31	35	21
41–56	20	32	50	39
57+	4	31	10	31
Total	100	100	100	100
Female				
0–12	12	17	14	21
13–32	34	26	31	29
33–40	50	22	38	17
41–56	3	16	15	18
57+	1	20	2	15
Total	100	100	100	100

Source: *Employment Gazette*, March 1991.

psychologist at the University of Manchester's Institute of Science and Technology, such behaviour is counter-productive.

'A gung-ho, go anywhere, work all hours attitude is pathetic. It's ineffective and not productive. Companies that encourage it are putting the health of their employees at risk', says Cooper. He advocates a forty- to fifty-hour week at most since his research suggests that after fifty hours workers' performance drops by 25%. After seventy hours, he says, they are contributing nothing.

Cooper emphasizes the impact of long working hours on families. Figures issued recently by the European Commission's statistical branch show that one in three British fathers work more than fifty hours. In West Germany, renowned for its work ethic, the figure is less than one in eight.

While most British firms remain unaware of the damage that prolonged stress can do, some are now addressing the problem. High technology companies such as Rank Xerox and IBM operate counselling schemes to help employees spot the danger signs, while some divisions of ICI give their entire workforce stress management training. This is not altruistic. The company wants to encourage balanced employees because they are more productive, so the reasons are completely mercenary.

But where does the balance lie? American psychologist Professor Janet Spence claims that there is nothing wrong in working hard as long as you have a good time. These 'enthusiasts', as she calls them, are the most productive. Workaholics, on the other hand, have a negative kind of black, addictive, driven quality. While there has been some anecdotal evidence that the last years of this century would herald a more relaxed attitude to business, overall successful entrepreneurs seem to work as hard as ever.

Acceptance of uncertainty

Managers in big business tend to seek to minimize risk by delaying decisions until every possible fact is known. This response to uncertainty is one that challenges the need to operate in the unknown. There is a feeling that to work without all the facts is not prudent or desirable.

Entrepreneurs have known that by the time the fog of uncertainty has been completely lifted, too many people will be able to spot the opportunity clearly. In point of fact an entrepreneur would usually only be interested in a decision that involved accepting a degree of uncertainty and would welcome, and on occasion even relish, that position.

Good health

Apart from being able to put in long days, the successful small-business owner needs to be on the spot to manage the firm every day. Owners are the essential lubricant that keeps the wheels of the small business turning. They have to turn their hands to anything that needs to be done to make the venture work and they have to plug any gaps caused either by other people's sickness or because they just cannot afford to employ anyone else for that particular job. They themselves cannot afford the luxury of sick leave. Even a week's holiday would be viewed as something of a luxury in the early years of a business life.

Self-discipline

One of the most common pitfalls for the novice business person is failing to recognize the difference between cash and profit. Cash can make people 'feel' wealthy and if it results in a relaxed attitude to corporate status symbols such as cars and luxury office fittings, then failure is just around the corner.

The owner-manager needs strong personal discipline to keep themselves and the business on the schedule the plan calls for. This is the drum beat that sets the timing for everything in the firm. Get that wrong and wrong signals are sent to every part of the business – both inside and out.

Other characteristics required of the small-business owner depend largely on the stage in the life cycle that the business has reached (see Figure 2.1).

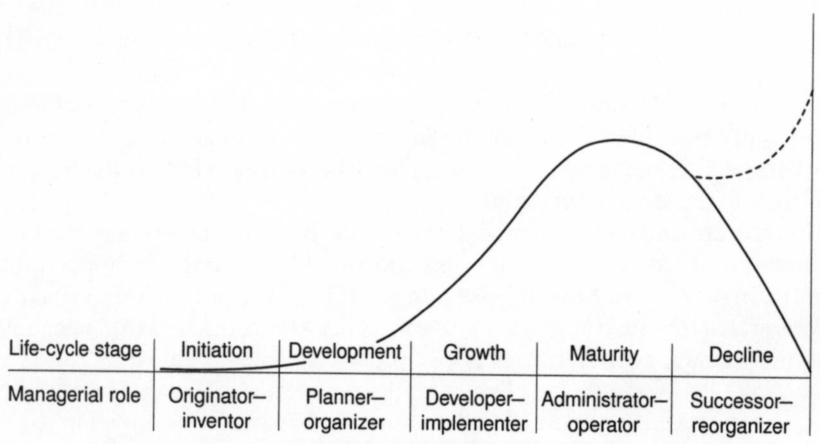

Figure 2.1 Managerial roles related to the life cycle of the firm (source: Carroll V. Kroeger, 'Managerial development in the small firm', *California Management Review*, **XVIII**, 1 (1974), p. 42).

Originator/inventor characteristics

Most people recognize innovation as the most distinctive trait of business founders. They tend to tackle the unknown; they do things in new and different ways; they weave old ideas into new patterns. But they go beyond innovation itself and carry their concept to market rather than remain in an ivory tower.

The high failure rate shows that small businesses are faced with many dangers. An essential characteristic of someone starting a business is a willingness to make decisions and to take risks. This does not mean gambling on hunches. It means carefully calculating the odds and deciding which risks to take and when to take them.

Small-business founders are rarely geniuses. There are nearly always people in their business who have more competence, in one field, than they could ever aspire to. But they have a wide range of ability and a willingness to turn their hands to anything that has to be done to make the venture succeed. They can usually make the product, market it and count the money, but above all they have the self-confidence that lets them move comfortably through uncharted waters.

Planner/organizer characteristics

Business founders need to be results oriented. Successful people set themselves goals and get pleasure out of trying to achieve them. Once a goal has been reached, they have to get the next target in view as quickly as possible. This restlessness is very characteristic. Sir James Goldsmith was a classic example, moving the base of his business empire from the United Kingdom to France, then to the United States – and finally into pure cash, ahead of the 1987 stock market crash.

James Gulliver, who built the Argyll group up to the fourth largest food retailer in the United Kingdom in around a decade, also exhibited this restless streak when he resigned in November 1987, still only in his fifties, to make a third 'fresh' start in his career.

To succeed the owner-manager needs both the ability and the willingness to make decisions – often involving unpleasant choices and always concerning matters of commercial life or death.

Unfortunately such decisions usually have to be taken without adequate information and without much 'professional' assistance.The ability to take irrevocable decisions on the basis of inadequate information is vital and any tendency to procrastination will waste more time than any 'one-person band' has available.

Later on when it becomes possible and appropriate to delegate decision-making, this situation will change. But in the early period the small-business owner's day is filled with large and small decisions.

The top entrepreneurs

Surprisingly, apart from anecdotal data, little is known about the nature of top entrepreneurs. Clearly some, such as Richard Branson, Alan Sugar, Anita Roddick and Petra Dorling (Cabouchon's founder) are well-known personalities, but most remain virtually unknown. For example, Barrie Haigh, who founded Innovex, was completely unknown to the public until he sold his private company in October 1996 for £550 million and was catapulted into the list of the country's most wealthy people.

Despite this, the entrepreneur has been viewed historically as a modern-day buccaneer who is bursting with new ideas, is highly enthusiastic, hyperactive, insatiably curious and whose talents have an exclusively genetic origin.

A study of the top 100 owner-managers just published by Sue Birley of The Cranfield School of Management and Liz Watson of Ernst & Young has for the first time cast some light on the profile of the British entrepreneur. Birley and Watson included in their study entrepreneurs with at least 20% of the shares in their company, who either founded the firm, or are a descendant of the founder and who continue to hold an executive position – a rigorous definition by any standards.

As there is no directory in the United Kingdom that ranks firms by the size of ownership, Birley and Watson had to carry out the laborious task of constructing their own. By searching through *Key British Enterprises, Kompass, Jordan's Growth Company Register* and similar directories, they put together a list of the 300 largest owner-managers' firms ranked by sales turnover. Company records were searched for ownership data, and fifty firms whose founders did not retain 20% of the shares were eliminated from the reckoning.

Since all industries were included in the search, it was important to take account of a variety of financial structures in trying to arrive at the 'top' firms. So the 250 remaining firms were also ranked by profit before tax and by net assets. The three ranks (turnover, profit and assets) were summed and a composite ranking produced.

This new list was circulated to forty partners within Arthur Young (the accounting firm, now Ernst & Young) throughout the country who had local knowledge of the relevant business sector. They were asked if they knew of any reason why the firm should not be included, or if there were any other firms that had been missed. This eliminated five firms – in one case the owner-manager had been fired by the investors for poor performance! The composition of the final list of the top 100 firms run by owner-managers is set out in Table 2.2.

Now to the nitty-gritty. Just what did Birley and Watson discover from their researching and questioning of these top British owner-managers?

Table 2.2 Profile of the top 100 firms

Industry sector	
Manufacturing	42%
Service	46%
Retail	12%
Location	
London and South-East	50%
Midlands and North	46%
Scotland	3%
Wales	1%
Northern Ireland	0%
Age of business	
Average	21 yrs
Youngest	4 yrs
Oldest	59 yrs
Ownership	
Average shareholding of owner-manager	44%
Number of employees	
Under 200	43%
Over 200	57%

A self-made man

Remarkably in a society characterized by widening educational opportunities and by government aid to business, a sample survey of this cadre of successful entrepreneurs revealed that they are almost entirely self-made, and almost entirely men: minimally educated, of average background, and driven by their own motivation.

At first glance, family background and parental employment would appear to be unexceptional. One might have expected such self-made, highly competent business people to have parents with managerial experience in large organizations. Yet most fit the traditional British entrepreneurial background in which they had gained some insight into self-employment.

While their mothers were primarily housewives, their fathers were, for example, shopkeepers, publicans, builders or farmers. Few had been employed in large organizations, and even fewer in positions of managerial responsibility.

Moreover, this entrepreneurial tradition was not confined to one member of the family – 39% of the entrepreneurs interviewed had siblings who also had their own firm.

This impression of purely personal drive is reinforced by a study of their educational qualifications. Only a handful had any post-school academic education. By far the greatest proportion had left the educational system with 'O' levels or their equivalent; 43% had left school at around the age of 16 and did not possess any further qualification.

Incidentally, that is a contrast with the United States, which has seen the emergence of a new breed of highly educated entrepreneurs. Of the American entrepreneurs examined in a survey of the 'Venture 1990', 48% came from the professional or managerial class, 72% had a first degree and 52% a postgraduate qualification. The position in the United Kingdom is starting to change as more ex-managers of large firms, who tend to have degrees and professional qualifications, are starting up or buying out their firms.

Mentors and advisers are crucial

Like most people, our entrepreneurs were primarily influenced by parents and teachers during their formative years. This close family network continued to be important during the formative years of their company, 70% of those surveyed describing either a member of their family or a close friend as the person who influenced them most at this time. Indeed, in those cases where the entrepreneur acknowledged a personal mentor, this was almost always a wife or father: 'I am essentially a loner: I have no single adviser as such. My wife was sympathetic and understanding when I started but she was never the "hostess". She is not materialistic or business oriented in the least, but I often bounce business ideas off her.' The remaining 30% saw themselves as entirely self-sufficient.

However, while the family continues to play an important role in the firm, the survey shows clearly that these successful entrepreneurs now rely upon those people who are closest to the business for advice and assistance – their bankers, accountants, lawyers and customers. The fourteen most useful sources of advice and assistance, as ranked by the 100 top British entrepreneurs, are listed in Table 2.3.

Table 2.3 Sources of advice and assistance

Rank
1. Accountants
2. Customers
3. Banks
4. Lawyer
5. Business contacts
6. Family
7. Friend
8. Suppliers
9. Consultants
10. Trade association
11. Local authority
12. Education institution
13. Enterprise institution
14. Chambers of commerce

The results seem to prove the adage that free advice is worth what you pay for it!

Conservatives to a man

Entrepreneurs are widely supposed to be supporters of Conservatism generally and Thatcherite economic policy specifically. But while the British entrepreneurs were very optimistic about prospects for the economy in the short term, and there was general approval of government attitudes towards business – variously described as 'very good', 'enlightened', 'incredibly switched-on' – there was little desire to influence or be involved in the formulation of policy.

When prompted, those in the survey made specific fiscal suggestions which focused narrowly on the reduction of tax – for example, 100% capital allowance in year one, tax relief on personal guarantees and genuine encouragement on stock option incentives.

Frequently, the entrepreneurs represented themselves as lying on the margins of the traditional City environment, interested only when wider developments came to affect their own position. Indeed, despite the fact that some were already quoted companies, the stock market crash of October 1987 was certainly not viewed as a disaster, although there was some concern about general business confidence and the ability to raise finance if necessary. Generally, the comments revealed an interesting mixture of personal pride (the effect was thought to be 'minimal on any well-run company') and latent hostility to City institutions ('helped to bring the City gents back to reality'). A survey of 200 owner managers carried out by Cranfield in 1996 largely endorsed these views and concerns. It was interesting to note that this group wanted Conservative policies to be implemented under Labour leadership.

The North/South divide

The profile of the British 100 seems to mirror a major economic shift which has been taking place in the United Kingdom. Exactly half of the firms came from the Midlands and northern England; only four firms were located in Scotland, one in Wales, and none in northern Ireland. Yet the ages of the firms indicate that this is not a recent phenomenon, but one that has been developing over the past thirty years.

There is further evidence to suggest that the popular division of economic England into unprofitable northern manufacturing firms and sleek southern service firms is mistaken. Yes, there is some concentration of manufacturing firms in the North and service firms in the South, but the well-publicized myth that manufacturing firms are based in Birmingham and service firms in Croydon does not necessarily hold.

Neither are service firms axiomatically more profitable, although there is some evidence that manufacturing firms take longer to grow, and that they dilute their ownership at a slower rate.

Exploding myths

The Birley/Watson study explodes the myth that British entrepreneurs are unable to manage successfully the growth of the firms that they founded. The firms in this group had all achieved substantial and successful growth. Nor do they fit the stereotype of the old-established family firm. All except one were founded post-war; the majority are a product of the 1960s and 1970s.

Moreover, success and growth are not confined to the high technology manufacturing firm, despite all political attempts to engineer industrial bias in this direction. Rather, success is clearly a function of a well-positioned, well-managed business, no matter what the industry.

So the firms run by top British entrepreneurs include sheet-metal workers and food production as well as the more glamorous computer firms; service companies range from employment agencies to haulage contractors to the more well-known retail cosmetics outlets. Cabouchon, one of the fastest growing firms started up in the 1990s, was founded by Petra Dorling, someone with no managerial experience. Yet within six years she had built a £200 million business, with worldwide distribution and growth still running at 145% compound.

Self-evaluation for prospective small-business owners

The following self-evaluation questions probe only those areas that are important to successfully starting up a business and can be controlled or affected by the individual. If the statement is rarely true, score 1; if usually true, score 2; and if nearly always true, score 3.

1. I know my personal and business objectives.
2. I get tasks accomplished quickly.
3. I can change direction quickly if market conditions alter.
4. I enjoy being responsible for getting things done.
5. I like working alone and making my own decisions.
6. Risky situations do not alarm me.
7. I can face uncertainty easily.

8. I can sell myself and my business ideas.
9. I have not had a day off sick.
10. I can set my own goals and targets and then get on with achieving them.
11. My family are right behind me in this venture – and they know it will mean long hours and hard work.
12. I welcome criticism – there is always something useful to learn from others.
13. I can pick the right people to work for me.
14. I am energetic and enthusiastic.
15. I do not waste time.

A score of 30+ is good; 20–30 is fair; below 20 is poor. A high score will not guarantee success but a low one should cause a major rethink.

Why small firms matter

Small businesses are a vital spark in the economy. Almost without exception throughout the 1980s and 1990s countries have sought ways and means to stimulate an increase in the numbers of small firms starting up in the economy. Their reasons for this concern are included in the list that follows.

Responsiveness to change

Being small and having limited resources, small firms are at the mercy of market falls. When economic conditions change, so must they. Large firms are not so nimble and can often continue in a direction not signalled or required by the economy for some time before recognizing the need for change.

For example, during the 1970s in the United Kingdom, the corner food store was universally recognized as being on the way out. The graphs showed the number of outlets contracting sharply and they were replaced by larger, less local and more efficient supermarkets. The major food retailers' vision was that virtually all purchasing would be confined to supermarkets and cash-and-carries on the edge of town. These arguments were supported by the increase in car and freezer ownership.

But suddenly during the late 1970s and 1980s this trend was sharply reversed. Arguments abound as to its cause. Popular mythology suggests that an influx of Asians from such countries as Uganda altered the economic equilibrium with their willingness, desire and necessity to work long hours and their ability to draw exclusively on family and friends who were prepared to work for a low wage.

But the central fact remains. The market had wanted and needed a strong local food shopping network, but big business had misread the signals. With their strong resources and less than flexible attitudes, big firms had been able to continue pursuing a strong-headed strategy for over a decade.

In the United States, for example, with its strong entrepreneurial bias, a quite different remedy was offered. When local shops were in danger of becoming uneconomic relative to larger competitors, they changed their format. They reduced their range to meet only major buying requirements, carrying only the top couple of brands of coffee, for example, rather than the eight to ten that supermarkets carry.

They also varied opening hours. Business format franchises came into the market, simplifying and routinizing procedures and thus making it easier for new people to enter the market. The fastest-growing retailer in the United States over this period was the Seven Eleven Store – a franchise that closely responded to the changing economic conditions and improved the flow of food at economic prices.

The United Kingdom, on the other hand, still suffers from the effect of leaving food retailing in the hands of a few large multiples. For example, food costs more because the supermarkets have higher margins than retailers in most other European countries and the United States.

A major source of innovation

Small businesses play a crucial role in creating new technology and products. During the last few decades the roles of large and small businesses in the development of new technologies and products have differed substantially. Large organizations are more likely to be sources of 'process' innovation. When they do develop new products, these tend to emerge from incremented improvements or refinements. Small business is more likely to strive for the unexpected, 'leap-frog' product innovations.[1]

Over 60% of the major inventions developed in the twentieth century were the work of independent inventors and small companies. So when you consider that small firms have historically accounted for only around 20% of output, it is clear that they are three times as 'effective' at innovating than are larger firms. Examples of such inventions include the airplane, the helicopter, catalytic oil refining, oxygen steel-making, photocopying, the automatic transmission, power steering, air conditioning, the Polaroid camera, the zipper and dacron-polyester fibre.[2] A study of 310 innovations developed between 1973 and 1975 showed that 24% were introduced by firms with fewer than 100 employees, and an additional 24% were developed by firms with between 100 and 999 employees.[3] More than half of today's inventors work outside the organized research groups of the corporate industrial laboratories.[4] Independent inventors took out roughly 40% of the total patents in the United States over the past twenty years. Of the 60% of patents held by corporations, one-third came from corporate employees working outside corporate laboratories.[5]

Firms with fewer than 1,000 employees produced innovation at about a quarter of the cost of middle-sized (1,000–10,000 employees) firms, and at about one-twenty-fifth that of large (more than 10,000 employees) firms.[6]

Small firms seem to encourage innovation because less restrictive organization provides for more individual initiative.[7] Four other reasons have been suggested. First, in a small technological firm, innovation is necessary to ensure survival, whereas the large firm tends simply to maintain its product market position. Second, managers of small technological companies (in which they often own a share) have more incentive to innovate. Third, large firms may prefer to hold technical improvements to a minimum for marketing reasons. Fourth, researchers and innovators in large firms tend to specialize; those in small firms tend to be technical generalists. Specialization can limit innovation; the more knowledge a developer has to draw on, the more original the resulting innovation tends to be.[8]

The conclusion to be drawn is that small businesses are a substantial source of innovation and technical change, and that they make their contribution more efficiently and at lower cost than larger businesses.

Job creation

Until the mid-1970s popular mythology had it that big businesses created most new jobs. That view was first seriously challenged by Professor David L. Birch of the Massachusetts Institute of Technology. His researchers disclosed that between 1969 and 1976 in the United States:

- Small businesses with twenty or fewer employees created 66% of all new jobs in the nation. In New England alone, such businesses created 99% of all new jobs.
- Mid-sized and big businesses created few new jobs.[9]

These conclusions were based on a study of the data files of 5.6 million businesses. To quote Professor Birch, 'it appears that the smaller corporations are aggressively seeking out most new opportunities, while the larger ones are primarily redistributing their operations'.[10]

Another US study found that small, young, high technology businesses create new jobs at a much faster rate than do older, larger businesses.[11]

Studies in France have confirmed that small firms were net creators of jobs throughout the 1970s, roughly absorbing the reduction in large firms' employment.

The overall job creation, in numbers of jobs, of firms employing fewer than and more than twenty people is compared in Table 2.4. This shows that the overall contribution of the smaller firms has varied much less across time – and hence across different stages of the economic cycle – than that of the larger firms. While it would be going too far, given the degree of comparability of the various studies, to assert that job generation by smaller firms is actually greater in times of recession, it is certainly more resilient to the effects of recession.

There are a number of possible reasons that this could be the case, but it must first be emphasized that this is not saying that small firms are immune to recession – they suffer the same effects as larger firms. Rather, it is implying that although there are obvious negative influences on small firms from recession, there are also some positive influences, which apply to a lesser degree, or not at all, to large firms. One such factor, for example, is that large firms may seek to withdraw from marginal or less profitable activities, leaving open niches for small firms either to provide specialized goods and services, or to operate in a local market. Large firms may also seek to subcontract peripheral activities such as cleaning and catering, offering opportunities for start-up or expansion of small businesses. Another factor is the possibility of significant numbers of people being made redundant by larger firms – or at least fearing the possibility – and setting up in business on their own account as an alternative response to the challenge of finding work. Some economies are more successful at job creation than others. According to *The Economist* (15–21 February 1997), America created 36 million new jobs over the twenty years to 1997, of which 31 million were in the private sector. Over the same period the European Union created only 5 million new jobs, of which only 1 million were in the private sector. The United Kingdom has been a conspicuous exception where almost all net new jobs have been created in small private sector firms at the expense of both large firms downsizing and the public sector shrinking.

A Cambridge (England) study[12] has suggested that much of the growth in importance of small firms is concentrated in the hands of very small firms employing only a handful of people. 'Larger' small businesses employing over twenty people have actually declined in number in the United Kingdom. The central problem which holds the key to future prospects is more in unlocking growth in established firms, than in simply starting new ones.

Table 2.4 Net job generation: comparison of time periods

	Size band		
Study period	1–19	20+	Total
1982–4	+1	–¾	+¼
1985–7	+½	0	+½
1987–9	+½	+½	+1

Source: *Employment Gazette*, November 1991.

Another study, by D. J. Storey,[13] concludes that this net job creation effect is confined to a tiny population of small firms. Storey's study of 774 surviving small firms concludes that over the decade to 1978 about 4% of those businesses that started would be expected to create 50% of employment generated. This conclusion is supported by other studies.[14]

However, knowing that these 'high flyers' exist and identifying them are two different tasks. One study, by C. Hakim 1989,[15] reports on the results of the aspirations for growth of 747,970 firms. Of these, 55% had no plans for growth, at a time when the economic climate was good. Looking more closely at Hakim's findings, it is evident that the typical 'no growth' firm is unincorporated, and is a home-based business with two or less employees, including the owner. Conversely, incorporated firms employing 10–24 people were nearly four times as likely to have fast growth aspirations.

Three other characteristics of 'high flyers' are their age and location and their willingness to take outside equity finance. One study[16] has shown that companies that either have or are willing to share equity with outsiders are more likely to grow than those that are reluctant.

There is also a near unanimous belief by researchers that younger firms grow more rapidly than older ones. The Superleague[17] study, drawn from a sample of the 3,489 UK companies that had grown turnover by 25% for two consecutive years to 1990, indicated that out of every hundred, sixty were registered after 1980 and only thirteen before 1970.

A further study[18] showed that for small service sector firms in six UK labour markets, three-quarters sold 75% or more of their service within their own locality. The strength or otherwise of those markets must have an important impact on rate of growth of small firms in the area.

There are mixed views as to whether sector or markets affect a firm's capacity to grow. Reynolds and Miller[14] also concluded that there is a positive relationship between this factor and growth rates, while another study[19] concluded that sector and market have no significant effect.

Why do people want to start a small business?

Advantages of running your own business

Few people get rich working for someone else. Running a business at least provides the opportunity to make more money, but whether you become wealthy depends very much on the success you make of it. If the business does well, the founder can determine the amount of money they take out as salary and can claim extra benefits on the firm (e.g. cars, pensions). Big businesses are only small businesses that succeed. If a business makes it to the big time, the founder might consider going public, which will dramatically increase the value of shares, or may decide to sell out for a large profit and retire in luxury.

More important than riches to many an entrepreneur, though, is the freedom that comes from being your own boss. Proprietors are totally independent and can plan the business and run it on a day-to-day basis in the way they want. It also gives them the opportunity to work in a field they really enjoy.

There are tax advantages too. Self-employed people have more allowances against income than employees. Directors of their own limited liability companies, however, are not classified as self-employed for tax purposes, but the benefits they can take from the company frequently mitigate their tax bills.

Disadvantages

Running a business is much more risky than working for someone else. If the business fails, you stand to lose far more than just your job. Not only will all your hard work have been to no avail, but you might suffer severe financial hardship if your business owes money since, as a self-employed person, you are personally liable to your debtors. This might mean selling your assets, including your home, and, at the worst, may result in bankruptcy. If you form a limited company your personal liability to creditors is limited to the value of the shares you hold – in theory. But, in practice, banks usually require a personal guarantee from the director(s) to secure an overdraft or loan for the business, which to some extent negates the benefits of limited liability status.

You are totally responsible for the success or failure of your business. This can be very exhilarating, but it is, inevitably, very stressful: constant pressure and long hours are par for the course for most entrepreneurs. This can drastically affect your social and family life, as well as your health.

To give a flavour of what it is like being your own boss, here in their own words are selected comments from some small-business founders.

> It gives you a feeling of being totally in control of your own destiny which is very exciting.

> You feel totally productive. You use your own time as you wish to spend it. Often this means working all hours of the day, six days a week – permanently. But it isn't a grind if you're doing it for yourself.

> I have earned far more in personal reward than I have financial benefits. It has given me self-confidence which has made me calmer, less neurotic and more prepared to take risks than hitherto.

> No longer being involved in office politics has given me an enormous feeling of freedom.

You get pleasure from the simplest things – just the fact that the office copier is working!

The ability to buy more and better material possessions is irrelevant compared to the sense of achievement you feel.

To begin with it's a very exciting feeling, you've stuck your flag in the sand. Then . . . there is a deadly pause while you sit and wait for the business to pour in. The bank manager/your spouse are going berserk and you wonder why you've done it. If you're sensible, you ride out this period by concentrating on planning the business properly and making sure you've got your costings right.

It's food for the soul.

It's good fun.

But . . .

It's very lonely knowing you are totally responsible for the success or failure of the business.

You have to be totally single-minded which can make you appear selfish to family and friends. It bust up my marriage.

You have to be prepared to turn your hand to anything that needs doing. A small firm can't afford all the back-up services – typing help, tea lady, mail boy – you might have become accustomed to as an employee.

Some aspects of the work are unpleasant – e.g. cold canvassing for clients, chasing up slow payers, and doing VAT returns.

You must develop a strong sense of responsibility to your staff. You can't be cavalier with them, after all, their career and jobs are in your hands.

You must be prepared to be ruthless, however friendly you are with staff or suppliers. If staff are no good, you must fire them. If suppliers let you down, get rid of them.

It was a great relief going back to being an employee since I no longer had the burden of finding staff salaries each week.

These days everyone is trying to live on credit so the biggest problem is cash flow.

It's very terrifying at the beginning. You sit there, waiting for the phone to ring, and when it does you hope like hell it's a potential customer rather than someone you owe money to.

The paperwork and form-filling is time-consuming and irritating. The

Department of Employment returned a form to us because we omitted to indicate the type of business of a client even though the client was called the Bank of America!

I find the responsibility a constant worry – it brings me out in cold sweats every night.

Despite the complaints, most business owners are pleased to have gone on their own and would have no hesitation in starting up another business rather than work for someone else.

In 1991 some 800 independent profitable companies with turnover of less than £25 million were asked what motivated them to start up and run their own businesses (see Figure 2.2).[20] The majority of the responses, 73.5%, had turnover between £1 million and £10 million. A massive 98% of responders rated personal satisfaction from success as an important motivator, with 70% of these rating it very important. Eighty-eight per cent rated 'ability to do things my own way' and 87% rated 'freedom to take a longer-term view' as important or very important, indicating that independence is a key motivator in entrepreneurs' minds.

Evidently, financial rewards register as an important motivator, but it is interesting to note that they are rated less highly than personal satisfaction,

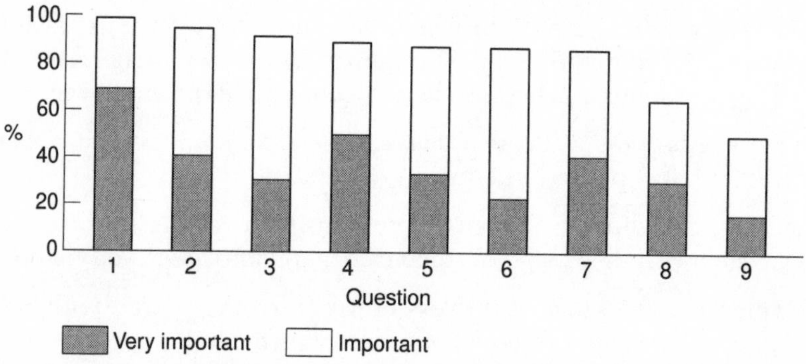

What do you consider are your principal motivations in running your business?

1 Personal satisfaction from success
2 Capital growth
3 Income
4 Ability to do things my own way
5 Freedom to take a longer-term view
6 Personal wealth
7 Security
8 Funds for retirement
9 Something to pass on to the children

Figure 2.2 Ranking of small-business motivation.

and only marginally more highly than independence. To assume, as some do, that owners of growing businesses are motivated purely by pecuniary gain is not only naive but also demonstrates a lack of understanding of entrepreneurs' personal goals.A very similar but smaller study reported on in 1996 came up with very similar findings.

Few were highly motivated by 'something to pass on to the children' – only 15% rated this as very important. Does the idea of a family company belong to the past?

How do small businesses measure success?

The same study echoes other studies that have revealed how small-business proprietors measure success in their business (see Figure 2.3).

Of the responder companies, 82% saw the quality of their product or service as a very important measure of business success – compared with 67% for pure financial performance. The message is clear, and is, in reality, common sense. Quality and customer service are the keys to long-term prosperity. It is the combination of quality and financial performance that provides the most acute measure of success.

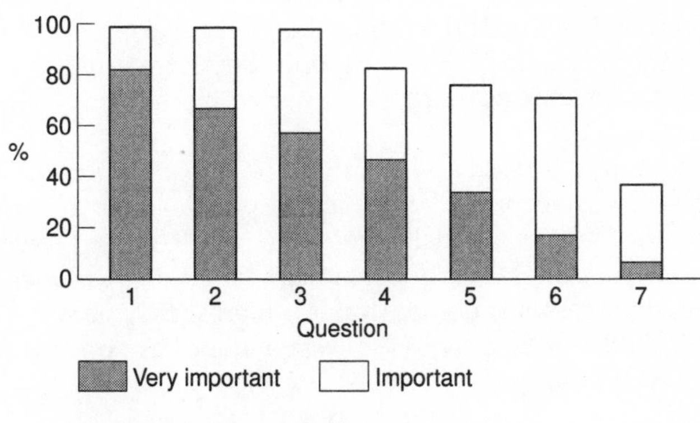

How do you measure success?

1 Quality of product/service
2 Financial performance
3 Development of an effective management team
4 Ability to sleep at night
5 Standing in industry
6 Balance of work/leisure
7 Standing in business community

Figure 2.3 Ranking of how small-business proprietors measure success.

Quality, of course, also reflects entrepreneurs' feelings of a job well done, matching the importance placed on personal satisfaction as a motivator.

Ego evidently plays little part in entrepreneurs' minds as only 8% rated 'standing in the business community' as a very important measure of success.

A developing business is only as good as the people involved in its development, so it is good to see that 98% of responders rated the development of an effective management team as an important or very important measure of success.

Challenges and problems

Running a small business may bring the potential for both personal satisfaction and conspicuous profit. But the path to both those goals is strewn with significant challenges and problems. Two studies capture the essence of these issues.

In 1990 at the Cranfield School of Management,[21] a study was conducted into the key problems perceived by the proprietors of small firms (see Table 2.5). Nearly 250 owner-manager firms replied to the survey and on average the firms employed around 25 people and had a turnover of around £2 million. The firms ranged from two to three years old upwards, with an average age of ten years.

Except in the very smallest of these companies, the greatest problem was generally seen as finding and keeping key staff. Larger small firms had problems finding a customer base to support their growth.

This view of problems was largely supported by the findings of the 1991 study (see Figure 2.4).[22]

Competition in this study was rated the most important challenge (changing places with recruiting and retaining people). More revealing is that the next two most important challenges were people related – recruitment/retention and management succession; once again the importance of people in developing businesses is demonstrated. Interestingly, family succession was seen as a challenge by only 31% of responders – as opposed to 83% for management succession.

Table 2.5 Problems in small businesses

No. of employees	Employing key staff	Finding customers	Raising new finance	High interest rates	Dealing with red tape
5 or less	56%	44%	50%	50%	38%
6–10	100%	30%	40%	20%	10%
11–20	86%	48%	33%	10%	10%
21-80	75%	84%	5%	16%	16%
80 or more	92%	58%	17%	17%	17%
Total	83%	59%	31%	27%	21%

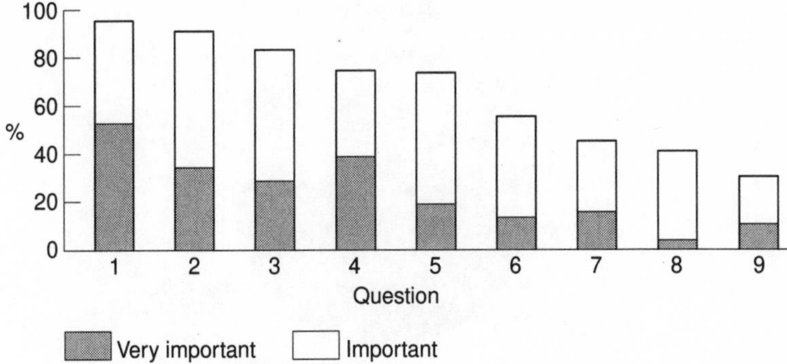

Over the next five years, what do you see as the most important challenges that you will face in managing the growth of your business?

1 Competition
2 Recruiting/retaining people
3 Management succession
4 New product development
5 Investment in new premises and equipment
6 Raising capital
7 Environmental considerations
8 Single European Market
9 Family succession

Figure 2.4 Ranking of the challenges facing small businesses.

In line with the response to 'contributors to growth', the Single European Market was rated a very important challenge by only 4% of responders.

Environmental considerations were not considered as great a challenge as might be expected, given the attention generally focused upon them. Only 16% of responders rated environmental considerations as a very important challenge.

Why do small firms fail?

Of the millions of new businesses born each year in the developed world, only half live as long as eighteen months and only one in five live as long as ten years.[23] These dramatic figures are often quoted, but are nevertheless open to question. In fact, no one really has defined failure. Many proprietors shut down because they are bored, can make more money elsewhere, have sold out to the competition, or have retired.[24]

A UK study[25] which confined itself to looking at business registered for VAT (i.e. had a turnover of around £25,000 or greater in 1990) came up with an interesting perspective on failure (see Figure 2.5). Only half the businesses

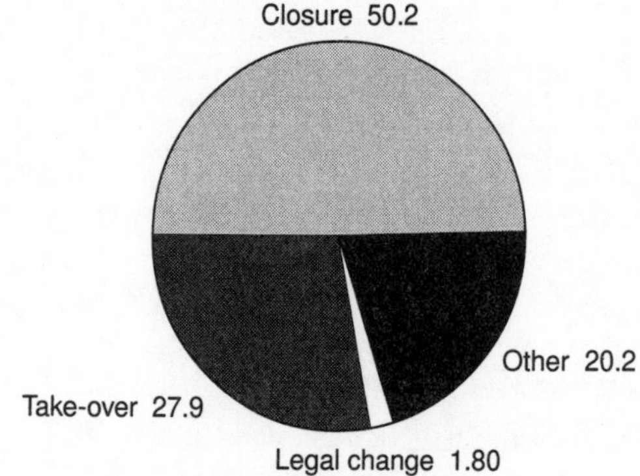

Figure 2.5 Reasons for small firms 'failing' (source: *Employment Gazette*, November 1990).

superficially recorded as 'failures' in the United Kingdom's national statistics, had actually ceased trading. Nearly a third had either changed their legal identity (i.e. become a company), or had been taken over by another business. However, the remaining fifth of small firms de-registered from VAT because they fell below the turnover threshold. (This is a sign that they are probably on their way to failure – but have not failed yet!)

The study concentrated on VAT returns as non-incorporated businesses do not file their accounts centrally.

Of the firms that do fail, the biggest single reason is incompetence. Disaster overtakes few, except perhaps in the eyes of the proprietor.

However you manage the statistics, many small businesses do go to the wall each year, which bears witness to the fact that running a business makes large demands, and that many people who start up are ill-equipped to do so. The highest risks are in the first few years.

Some of these budding entrepreneurs lose their life savings, others end up in endless debt. A fortunate few lose only their dignity and rise phoenix-like a few years later, using their experience as a base on which to build a successful venture.

Some academics believe the high failure rate is the price that has to be paid in order to produce a thriving new business sector – the survival of the fittest.

There is no risk-free way to a profitable business but it is as well to know the dangers that lie ahead.

New start-up businesses fail for the following eleven basic reasons:[26]

1. *Lack of expertise.* Starting a business from scratch calls for remarkable versatility. The owner-manager types the invoices with one finger in the evenings, does the books at the weekend, sells on Monday, makes the goods from Tuesday and delivers when they can. People with a history in large firms sometimes find it difficult to become a jack of all trades.

2. *No product/marketing strategy.* Until you have defined who will buy your product or service, and why, you shouldn't begin to offer it.
3. *Over-optimism about market size.* It is a fundamental misconception to believe that people are simply sitting waiting to be sold to. New businesses need to conduct research into the market they are aiming at, to see who the competitors are and make some reasoned estimate of what their anticipated sales will be.
4. *Underestimating the start-up time.* There is often a great deal to do before the customers come along – premises to be found and fitted out, equipment and stock to be bought. Estimate how long you think it will take, double it, and add on a bit more.
5. *Lack of working capital.* If you have not calculated 3 and 4 correctly you could easily run out of money. Scarce cash is tied up, and money is flowing in one direction only until customers start buying in reasonable numbers. Assess your capital requirements with a good safety margin at the outset. A well-prepared cash flow forecast will help you decide how much is needed and when.
6. *Start-up cost too high.* New businesses should be lean and mean. Do not spend too much on fixtures, fittings and equipment too soon. People with a background in big business often start with extravagantly high standards. They expect an electronic typewriter and photocopier close to hand, and to sit in an executive-style office from the outset. These overheads have to be spread across the products/service sold and you can lose your competitive edge by being too greedy.
7. *Consequences of early growth.* Many people think their problems are over once customers start to roll in – but they may have only just begun. A business changes its shape and size very rapidly in its early days. As sales grow, ever increasing sums of cash are needed to fuel that growth. And the danger is overtrading, i.e. growing faster than cash resources allow.
8. *Mistaking cash for profit.* The cash that flows into the business has not had any of the automatic deductions knocked off it as has a pay cheque from an employer. Too often entrepreneurs yield to the temptation to use this cash to maintain their living standards, and when the bills come in – from the suppliers, for National Insurance, for VAT – they cannot pay them. The Inland Revenue and Customs & Excise put more businesses into liquidation than anyone else.
9. *Wrong location.* Where you conduct your business and how much rent you pay is vital. Do not be tempted to take premises just because the rent is cheap – no customers may pass that way. Equally, do not take on an expensive high street site if your business turnover is unlikely to cover the costs. Your initial market research should help you identify a suitable location.

10. *Selecting and managing people.* Big companies can afford to make the odd mistake when selecting staff. Small businesses cannot afford to get it wrong.
11. *No management accounts.* New business people often see regular accounting as a bureaucratic nonsense carried out for the benefit of the Inland Revenue alone. For them the end of the first year is often the end of the business.

County Natwest Wood Mac, the investment arm of the Natwest Bank, has scrutinized the forty-five companies quoted on either the Unlisted Securities Market of the now defunct Third Market, where administrators or administrative receivers were appointed in 1989 and 1990. Philip Augar, head of research at County Natwest Wood Mac, claims that the reasons for failure in these relatively large small firms is just the same as in really small firms, but writ large. He also suggests that all the 'symptoms of collapse' can be seen from the report and accounts issued to shareholders. The following are the warning signs that Augar identified:

- *Is the chairman also the chief executive or managing director?* More than 60% of the companies that failed had a combined chairman and chief executive or an executive chairman with no separate chief executive or managing director. The same argument also holds good in unquoted companies where the roles of MD and of the functional roles, for example finance or marketing director, are also held by one person. With smaller companies with few staff, the question to ask is: does the boss have too many jobs?
- *Is gearing more than 100%?* Gearing is a company's debt measured as a percentage of shareholders' funds, excluding goodwill and other intangibles. Debt far greater than equity can prove a fatal liability in recessions when cash is king. Has gearing increased significantly since last year? Attempts to borrow a way out of trouble may become frenzied in the final months, and the policy often fails.
- *Are short-term borrowings larger than long-term borrowings?* In eighteen of the failed USM companies, over 80% of their corporate debt was due to be repaid within a year of the date of collapse.

  Small-business people today might do well to ponder on why they took out short-term loans in the first place. Younger managers may not have realized that, traditionally, bank finance was regarded in Britain only as a transitional or seasonal device to finance fluctuations in working capital, and that for at least part of the year, businesses would have expected to be in credit. The notion that permanent finance should be obtained from banks and linked to short-term interest rates came over from America in the 1970s, and is a thoroughly bad idea.

  It had superficial attractions, such as that firms would not be scrutinized so thoroughly and would not be prey to expensive venture capitalists.

There was also a perception that, in a crunch, real interest rates would go negative (often minus 5% or more in periods of high inflation); if you sat tight, the problem would shrink in real terms. These days, with the United Kingdom locked into low inflation policies and a structure of positive real interest rates, if borrowers sit tight, the problem simply gets worse through the remorseless mathematics of compound interest.

- ☐ *Has turnover grown at more than 50% per annum over the last five years?* This was the average increase in business by all the failed companies in 1989–90, while almost a fifth of them doubled turnover that year. Rapid expansion can lead to overtrading where companies just do not have the ready cash to pay their bills although order books are full.
- ☐ *Has the company recently made, or is it planning to make, a major move of premises?* The final accounts for both Bestwood and Reliant, two of the failures in the Wood Mac survey, showed reorganization costs as extraordinary items. Almost all the companies we know that have moved premises, for whatever reason, have experienced a one- to three-year profit set-back.
- ☐ *Have any directors resigned?* Annual reports for more than half the failed companies show resignations from the board. Five directors left British & Commonwealth, for instance. Directors who have sold large tranches of their own shares also do not inspire confidence in the company.
- ☐ *Are the report and accounts rather lavish?* Bad news is sometimes concealed by glossy packaging. Yellowhammer, for instance, produced a two-volume brochure with its final report; Polly Peck went for a large non-standard format.
- ☐ *Is the company in a cynical industry?* Building and property development, advertising and finance were identified as high risk.

If you are assessing a potential acquisition, a competitor or your own company and the answer is 'yes' to more than five of these questions, County Natwest Wood Mac advises you to proceed with caution; if more than eight, expect the worst.

Which businesses are most likely to fail?

A simple if crude method of discovering which businesses are most likely to fail is to see which sectors have the largest consistent proportion of failures. Table 2.6 shows, by way of example, the percentage of company liquidations by industrial sector, as calculated by the Department of Trade and Industry.

As you can see, 16.2% of all failures came from the construction industry, followed by business services at 10.4%, metals and engineering at 6.5% and transport and communication at 6.2%.

Table 2.6 Company liquidations in England and Wales. Industrial analysis – percentages

Industry	1983	1990
Agriculture/horticulture	0.6	0.7
Manufacturing		
Food, drink and tobacco	0.6	0.7
Chemicals	0.9	0.6
Metals and engineering	11.3	6.5
Textiles and clothing	8.7	6.1
Timber and furniture	2.2	2.6
Paper, printing and publishing	3.4	3.7
Other	4.0	5.3
Total	31.1	25.5
Construction	13.2	16.2
Transport and communication	6.4	6.2
Wholesaling		
Food, drink and tobacco	1.8	1.6
Motor vehicles	0.7	0.7
Other	7.8	4.8
Retailing		
Food, drink and tobacco	1.4	1.6
Motor vehicle and filling stations	3.4	1.2
Other	11.7	7.8
Financial institutions	1.3	2.0
Business services	11.0	10.4
Hotels and catering	3.0	3.2
All other	7.0	18.0
Total	100.0	100.0

As well as identifying those sectors with a high failure propensity, it is also worth discovering in which sectors the growth in failure rates is accelerating (see Figure 2.6).

Over the twelve months to the end of 1990, the construction industry has seen a greater than 95% increase in failure level, while failures in the textile industry were a mere 35% or so higher.

Business failures in perspective

Before becoming too depressed by the headlines reporting record company failures, it is worth remembering that there are far more businesses trading now than there were five or even ten years ago. Table 2.7 shows the 'real' overall position in terms of failures as a proportion of active companies. You can see that 1.8% of registered companies failed in the first quarter of 1991,

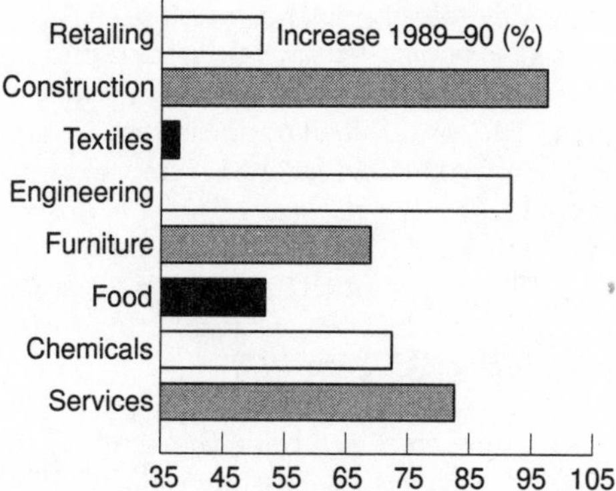

Figure 2.6 Failures by sector (source: *Trade Indemnity*).

Table 2.7 Ratio of company insolvencies to number of companies registered

Ratio to active register (%)		Ratio to active register (%)	
1986	1st q. 1.8	1989	1st q. 1.0
	2nd q. 1.8		2nd q. 1.1
	3rd q. 1.8		3rd q. 1.1
	4th q. 1.8		4th q. 1.1
1987	1st q. 1.7	1990	1st q. 1.2
	2nd q. 1.6		2nd q. 1.2
	3rd q. 1.5		3rd q. 1.4
	4th q. 1.4		4th q. 1.8
1988	1st q. 1.3	1991	1st q. 1.8
	2nd q. 1.2		
	3rd q. 1.1		
	4th q. 1.1		

which was the tail end of a recession, the same proportion as failed in the first quarter of 1986 – the tail end of the last mild UK recession – so it really is not accurate to describe the current failure rates as 'the worst ever'.

References

1. Krasner, O. J. and Dubrow, M. L., 'The role of small business in research and development, technological change and innovation in region IX', in S. W. Hentzell (ed.), *The Environment for Small Business and Entrepreneurship in Region IX* (Menlo Park, CA: SRI International for the SBA, 1979).
2. Smollen, Leonard E. and Levin, Molly Apple, 'The role of small business in research and development, technological change and innovation in region IX', in Jeffry A. Timmons (ed.), *A Region's Struggling Savior: Small Business in New England* (Walthma, MA: SBANE Foundation, for the SBA, 1979), p. 74.

3. Smollen and Levin, 'The role of small business', p. 75.
4. Storey, D. J., *The Small Firm on International Survey* (London: Croom Helm, 1983).
5. Krasner and Dubrow, 'The role of small business', p. 100.
6. Smollen and Levin, 'The role of small business', pp. 75–9.
7. Doctors, Samuel I., and Wokutch, Richard E., 'Impact of state and local policies', in Paul W. Houck (ed.), *The Status of Small Business in Region 111* (University Park, PA: Pennsylvania Technical Assistance Program for the SBA, 1979), pp. 11–17.
8. Smollen and Levin, 'The role of small business', p. 80.
9. Birch, David L., *The Job Generation Process* (Cambridge, MA: MIT Programme on Neighborhood and Regional Change, 1979).
10. Ibid., p. 103.
11. US Department of Commerce, *Recommendations for Creating Jobs Through the Success of Small Innovative Businesses* (Washington, DC: US Government Printing Office, March 1980).
12. Alan Hughes, *Industrial Concentration and the Small Business Sector in the UK: The 1980s in historical perspective*, University of Cambridge Working Papers, 1990.
13. Storey, D. J., 'Manufacturing employment changes in northern England 1965–78: The role of small business', in D. J. Storey (ed.), *Small Firms in Regional Economic Development* (Cambridge: Cambridge University Press, 1985).
14. Reynolds, P. D. and Miller, B., *1988 Minnesota New Firms Study: An exploration of New Firms and their Economic Contribution* (Minneapolis, MN: Centre for Urban and Regional Affairs, 1988).
15. Hakim, C., 'Identifying fast growth in small firms', *Employment Gazette*, January 1989, pp. 29–41.
16. Hall, G., 'Lack of finance as a constraint on the expansion of innovatory small firms', in J. Barber, J. S. Metcalf and M. Porteous (eds), *Barriers to Growth in Small Firms* (London: Routledge, 1989).
17. 3Is/Cranfield European Enterprise Centre (1990) *Superleague Companies* (Cranfield, England).
18. Curran, J., Blackburn, R., and Woods, A., 'Profiles of the small enterprise in the service sector', paper presented at the University of Warwick, 18 April 1991.
19. Storey, D. J., Keasey, K., Watson, R. and Wunarez, P., *The Performance of Small Firms: Profits, Jobs and Failures* (London: Croom Helm, 1987).
20. Coopers & Lybrand, *Motivating Entrepreneurs*, July 1991.
21. Colin Barrow, *Key Staff Recruitment in Small Firms in the United Kingdom*, Cranfield Working Papers (Cranfield, England, 1990).
22. Coopers & Lybrand, July 1991.
23. Aicola Siropolis, *A Guide to Entrepreneurship* (New York: Houghton Mifflin, 1982).
24. Albert Shapiro, 'Numbers that lie', *Inc*, May 1981.
25. 'The 1990s decade of growth in enterprise', *Employment Gazette*, November 1990.
26. Gillian Clegg and Colin Barrow, *How to Start and Run Your Own Business* (London: Macmillan, 1984).

3

Forming the business

Throughout most of the developed world three main types of legal forms are used predominantly to run small business organizations. These forms are as follows:

- Sole traderships, where generally only one person funds the business activities.
- Partnerships, where two or more people band together to finance or run a venture.
- Corporations/limited companies, where it is possible for many thousands to subscribe for a share in business ownership and, in theory at least, in its governance and direction.

The cooperative is a fourth and minority legal form, which nevertheless has a part to play in the small-business world in some countries.

The relative position of each of the three main forms of business, which themselves account for more than 95% of organized business, can be ascertained from Figure 3.1 showing the position at the start of the 1990s in the United Kingdom, which remains broadly similar today and is fairly typical of the position in other advanced economies. Within these general figures are some wide variations. For example, according to research by Barclays Bank,[1] start-ups are much more likely to be sole traders (60%) than companies (20%). Also women are less likely to start companies than are men (10% vs. 25%).

Sole trader

The vast majority of new businesses set up each year in the United Kingdom choose to do so as sole traders. The form has the merit of being relatively

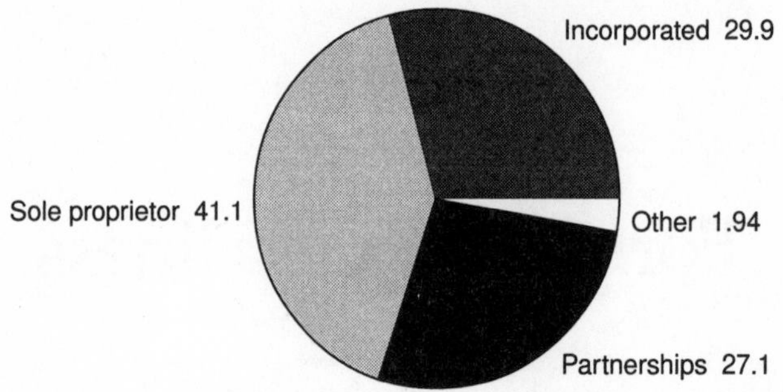

Figure 3.1 UK businesses registered for VAT by form of organization, per cent (source: *Employment Gazette*, November 1990).

formality-free and, unless you intend to register for VAT, there are no rules about the records you have to keep. There is no requirement for your accounts to be audited, or for financial information on your business to be filed at Companies House.

As a sole trader there is no legal distinction between you and your business – your business is one of your assets, just as your house or car is. It follows from this that if your business should fail, your creditors have a right not only to the assets of the business, but also to your personal assets, subject only to the provisions of the Bankruptcy Acts (these allow you to keep only a few absolutely basic essentials for yourself and family).

It is possible to avoid the worst of these consequences by ensuring that your private assets are the legal property of your spouse, against whom your creditors have no claim. (You must be solvent when the transfer is made, and that transfer must have been made at least two years prior to your business running into trouble.) However, to be effective such a transfer must be absolute and you can have no say in how your spouse chooses to dispose of his or her new-found wealth!

The capital to get the business going must come from you – or from loans. There is no access to equity capital, which has the attraction of being risk-free. In return for these drawbacks you can have the pleasure of being your own boss immediately, subject only to declaring your profits on your tax return. (In practice you would be wise to take professional advice before doing so.)

Although there is nothing that you are required to do legally as a sole trader, it is sensible to do the following:

- □ Open a separate bank account for the business.
- □ Tell your local tax inspector (or get an accountant to do so). The inspector will give you some indication of allowable business expenses.
- □ Take out full insurance cover against possible loss or damage to any equipment – if you have invested in any.

- ☐ Take out a personal injury/illness insurance since your National Health Insurance will not cover you if you are injured or ill while operating your own business.

The advantages and disadvantages of being a sole trader are as follows:

Advantages

- ☐ Easy to set up – you can start the business in a small way, from your home if you want.
- ☐ You are the boss. You can run the business at your own pace and in your own way.
- ☐ You keep the profits.
- ☐ You can offset some business expenses against earnings for tax purposes.
- ☐ No public disclosure of your affairs.
- ☐ Profit or loss in one trade can be set off against profit and loss in any other business you run – or past PAYE.

Disadvantages

- ☐ You are totally responsible for any debts that your business incurs. If you go bankrupt, your creditors are entitled to seize and sell your possessions – personal as well as business.
- ☐ It can be lonely.
- ☐ You have a low status.

Most countries have sole tradership as a legal structure in the way described here. Some countries have variations on the same theme. For example, in France where nearly 70% of all active businesses are operated as sole traderships, husbands and wives may be jointly responsible. In the United Kingdom husbands and wives would need to form either a partnership or a limited company to share the 'ownership' of a venture.

Partnerships

Partnerships are effectively collections of sole traders and, as such, share the legal problems attached to personal liability. There are very few restrictions to setting up in business with another person (or persons) in partnership, and several definite advantages. By pooling resources you may have more capital; you will be bringing, hopefully, several sets of skills to the business; and if you are ill, the business can still carry on.

There are two serious drawbacks that merit particular attention. First, if your partner makes a business mistake, perhaps by signing a disastrous contract, without your knowledge or consent, every member of the partnership must shoulder the consequences. Under these circumstances your personal assets could be taken to pay the creditors even though the mistake was no fault of your own.

Second, if your partner goes bankrupt in his or her personal capacity, for whatever reason, his or her share of the partnership can be seized by his or her creditors. As a private individual you are not liable for your partner's private debts, but having to buy them out of the partnership at short notice could put you and the business in financial jeopardy. Even death may not release you from partnership obligations and in some circumstances your estate can remain liable. Unless you take 'public' leave of your partnership by notifying your business contacts, and advertising your retirement in the *London Gazette* you will remain liable indefinitely.

The legal regulations governing this field are set out in the Partnership Act 1890, which in essence assumes that competent business people should know what they are doing. The Act merely provides a framework of agreement which applies 'in the absence of agreement to the contrary'. It follows from this that many partnerships are entered into without legal formalities – and sometimes without the parties themselves being aware that they have entered a partnership!

- ☐ The main provisions of the Partnership Act are as follows:
- ☐ All partners contribute capital equally.
- ☐ All partners share profits and losses equally.
- ☐ No partner shall have interest paid on their capital.
- ☐ No partner shall be paid a salary.
- ☐ All partners have an equal say in the management of the business.

It is unlikely that all these provisions will suit you so you would be well advised to get a 'partnership agreement' drawn up in writing by a solicitor, at the outset of your venture.

Why you might consider a partnership

- ☐ As a means of starting up with increased capital (presuming that both you and your partners put money in).

- ☐ You might not feel confident to start a business entirely on your own and would prefer to share the responsibilities with someone else.
- ☐ You have complementary skills – one of you may have specialist skills and the other management flair, or one the money, the other the ideas.

Choosing a partner

If the business is going to have any chance of success, it is essential that the partners trust each other and can work together harmoniously. Also, since you and your partner(s) have unlimited financial liability for the firm, if things go wrong – regardless of whose fault it is – creditors can claim the personal possessions of each and every partner. A partnership is therefore almost as close a relationship as a marriage. So the choice of partner must be made with as much care as selecting a wife or husband.

If you are considering a partnership, ask yourself first if you have the right temperament to be a partner. Some people are too individual to be able to cope with pooling their ideas and resources on an equal footing, as the case that follows illustrates.

EXAMPLE 3.1

Eric O'Keefe opted out of the highly successful Spanish bar that he had painstakingly set up and nurtured for seven years within a year of taking a partner. He took the partner because he needed finance to expand, Eric could not tolerate what he saw as the partner's 'interference' with the way the bar was run. He now admits – with hindsight – that the partner was perfectly entitled to express his views on what had, after all, become a joint project. Eric agrees that his personality was the problem. 'I'm better off on my own,' he admits and, perhaps equally significantly, 'alcohol always causes personality clashes but it's the only business I would contemplate working in.'

There are no hard-and-fast rules about selecting a partner, but the most successful partnerships do seem to be those where the partners have known each other for some time – either as friends or business associates – and where they have complementary skills and personalities. For instance, one partner may be a technical person who looks after the manufacturing side of the operation while the other is good at dealing with people and looks after sales, or the combination may be of an 'ideas' person with a down-to-earth practical person who can implement the ideas.

Partnership agreements

As already stated, the provisions of the Partnership Act apply if there is no other agreement between the partners, but it is sensible, if not essential, to get a solicitor to draw up a Deed of Partnership between you and your partners. You may want to vary the rules laid down in the Partnership Act and to cover points not mentioned. This document also regulates exactly how the business is run. It should cover the following:

- *Profit sharing.* If, for example, one partner has sunk more capital into the business than the other, profits will not be shared in equal proportions; or you might decide to distribute profits according to the number of contracts completed, the number of hours worked, or by some other method.
- *Withdrawing money.* It is important to limit the amount of money that each partner can take out of the business each month otherwise you may find you have insufficient working capital.
- *Time off.* The length and frequency of holidays should be laid down, as well as what rules apply if a partner is incapacitated through illness. They will be entitled to their share of the profits, so you may consider it important to stipulate a time limit after which the partnership can be dissolved.
- *Voting rights.* Unless the agreement states otherwise, all partners have equal voting rights. You might wish to vary this.
- *Duration of partnership.* How long do you want your partnership to last – one, three, five or ten years? Or you might prefer it to be for an indefinite period, terminating after, say, three months' notice.
- *Admitting or expelling a partner.* The consent of every partner is necessary before a new partner can be admitted. If you want the right to have a relative, e.g. your son, admitted as a partner later, this should be stated in the agreement. Unless the agreement states otherwise, you must get a court order if you want to expel a partner, so the partnership deed should set out in detail the circumstances in which a partner can be expelled.
- *Dissolving or rescinding the partnership.* Dissolution will occur automatically on the death or bankruptcy of a partner – unless the partnership agreement provides otherwise. If you discover that your partner has given you false information you may apply to the court to rescind the partnership agreement.
- *Getting capital out.* When dissolution occurs, a partner is entitled to have the partnership property sold and all assets distributed. After the assets have been realized and outstanding debts paid, any surplus must be distributed among the partners in equal shares – unless you make a different arrangement in the partnership deed.

  The proceeds from the sale of assets must be applied in the following order, although, again, the partnership deed can vary this:

(a) payment to creditors who are not partners;
(b) repaying loans made by partners;
(c) paying back partners their capital contribution;
(d) surplus divided among partners.

If there are not enough assets, partners must make up the deficiency in the proportions in which they shared profits.

- *Notice of withdrawal from a partnership.* The agreement should state how much notice should be given to each of the other partners if one partner wants to withdraw. Remember, if you are withdrawing, that you are still responsible for all obligations which your firm incurred while you were a partner. Give notice to all customers and suppliers that you are withdrawing and make sure that your name is removed from all stationery. Advertise the fact in the *London Gazette.*
- *Conflicting interests.* Partners are free to engage in other business activities unless the partnership agreement prohibits this. However, no partner may engage in any activity that competes with the partnership business. It might be sensible to provide limited partnerships.

Limited partnerships

A partner who is prepared to put capital (or property of a stated amount) into the business but who wants no part in running it can protect themselves against liability for debts or obligations of the partnership beyond the amount that he or she has contributed by registering a limited partnership with the Registrar of Companies. Such a person is usually referred to as a 'sleeping partner' and is prohibited by law from taking part in the management of the business, from making contracts or drawing cheques on the firm's account (Limited Partnership Act 1907 applies).

Advantages

- No formalities involved in setting up (although it is sensible to have a partnership deed drawn up between you).
- Less lonely than starting up totally on your own (in theory anyway!).
- Secrecy – no obligation to submit copies of your accounts for public scrutiny.
- A chance to start off with increased capital.
- No limitations on capital, assets or scope of business as with a limited company.

Disadvantages

- Each partner is liable for the debts of the company – regardless of which partner is at fault.

- □ Risk of personality clashes between partners.
- □ The death or bankruptcy of any partner automatically dissolves a partnership unless there is an agreement otherwise.

Once again, the partnership is a usually recognized business form, with some variations applying in different countries. In Italy, for example, unlimited liability companies exist as a vehicle for accommodating the partnership concept.

Limited companies

Limited liability companies

In the United Kingdom, before the 1895 Companies Act, it was necessary to have an Act of Parliament or a Royal Charter in order to set up a company. Now, out of the 3.5 million businesses registered in the United Kingdom, over 1 million are limited companies, although it must be said that a number of newly registered companies never trade.[2] As the name suggests, in this form of business your liability is limited to the amount that you contribute by way of share capital.

A company registered in accordance with the Companies Acts is a separate legal entity, distinct from both its shareholders, directors and managers. The liability of the shareholders is limited to the amount paid or unpaid on issued share capital. A company has unlimited life and no limit is placed on the number of shareholders. The Companies Act does, however, place many restrictions on the company. It must maintain certain books of account, appoint an auditor and file an annual return with the Registrar of Companies which includes the accounts as well as details of directors and mortgages.

A minimum of two shareholders and one director is required to form a company. There are in fact two types of company limited by shares. The first is a 'public' company (plc) which has a minimum authorized and allotted share capital of £50,000. This is a company that, according to its Memorandum of Association, may invite the public to subscribe for its shares. Any company that is not 'public' is called 'private'. 'Public' companies have further onerous, legal requirements and restrictions placed upon them. Generally, most companies start life as 'private' and only become 'public' when they need funds from a wider range of shareholders. Companies pay 'corporation tax' on their taxable profits.

The 1981 Companies Act and subsequent Acts allow some concessions to small and medium-sized companies, in terms of the amount of information to be reported. So, for example, some small firms produce only a very limited balance sheet and virtually no profit and loss account. These relaxations are intended to make life easier for small firms with restricted access to financial advice. However, in practice only a very unwise entrepreneur would run a business without comprehensive data.

Advantages of the limited company

- Members' (the directors and shareholders) financial liability is limited to the amount of money they have paid for shares.
- The management structure is clearly defined, which makes it easy to appoint, retire or remove directors.
- If extra capital is needed, it can be raised by selling more shares privately.
- It is simple to admit more members.
- The death, bankruptcy or withdrawal of capital by one member does not affect the company's ability to trade.
- The disposal of the whole or part of the business is easily arranged.
- High status.

Disadvantages

- Requirement to register the company with the Registrar of Companies and provide annual returns and accounts – which must be audited. All details of the company are available for public inspection so there can be no secrecy. There are penalties for failing to make returns.
- Can be more expensive to set up.
- May need professional help to form.
- As a director you are treated as an employee and must pay tax through PAYE and Class 1 National Insurance contributions both as an employee and as an employer.
- The advantages of limited liability status are increasingly being undermined by banks, finance houses, landlords and suppliers who require personal guarantees from the directors before they will do business.

Requirements for a private limited company

1. *A registered business name.* This must be followed by the word 'Limited' or 'Ltd' ('Cyfngedig' may be used instead if the company has a registered office in Wales). The Companies Registration Office exercises some control over the choice of name – it cannot be identical (or very similar to)

the name of an existing company. It will not be considered if it is offensive or illegal and the use of certain words in a company (e.g. 'Institute', 'International') can only be used in certain circumstances. The company name must be displayed in a conspicuous place at every office, or other premises where the company carries out business.

2. *A registered office.* This need not necessarily be the same address as the one from which the business is conducted. Quite frequently the address used for the registered office is that of the firm's solicitor or accountant. This is the address, however, where all official correspondence will go. EEC regulations now require the name of the company to be prominently displayed.
3. *Shareholders.* There must be a minimum of two shareholders (also described as 'members' or 'subscribers'). There must be at least one director and a separate individual as company secretary. In small companies these are usually the two shareholders (often husband and wife) but the directors and secretary do not necessarily have to be shareholders. A private company can have up to fifty shareholders.
4. *Share capital.* The company must be formed with a stated, nominal share capital divided into shares of fixed amounts. Small companies are frequently formed with nominal share capital of £100.
5. *Memorandum of Association.* The Memorandum is the company's charter. It states the company's name; the situation in Great Britain of its registered office, i.e. England, Scotland, Wales (but not the town); its share capital; the fact that liability is limited and, most importantly, the objects for which the company has been formed. In theory, the company can only operate in the areas mentioned in the objects clause but in practice the clause is drawn to cover as wide an area as possible, and anyway a 75% majority of the members of the company can change the objects whenever they like. Nevertheless, it is worth bearing in mind that directors of the company will incur personal liability if the company engages in a type of business that is not authorized by the objects clause. The Memorandum must be signed by at least two shareholders.
6. *Articles of Association.* This document contains the internal regulations of the company – the relationship of the company to its shareholders and the relationship between the individual shareholders. Many companies do not bother to draw up their own Articles but adopt (sometimes with some modification) Articles set out in Table A of the 1948 Companies Act, which are quite satisfactory for the majority of private companies. The Articles must be signed by the initial shareholders.
7. *Certificate of Incorporation.* This is the document that the Registrar of Companies issues to you once he or she has approved your choice of name and your Memorandum. When you receive this document, your company legally exists and is ready to trade.

8. *Auditors.* Every company must appoint a qualified auditor. The auditor's duty is to report to the treasurer whether the books of the company have been properly kept, and whether the balance sheet and profit and loss account presents (or does not present) a true and fair view of the company's affairs and complies with the Companies Acts. Auditors are appointed or reappointed at general meetings at which annual accounts are presented, and they hold office from the conclusion of that meeting until the next general meeting.
9. *Accounts.* The Companies Act lays down strict rules on accounting. Every company must maintain a set of records which show the financial position at any one time with reasonable accuracy. The accounts comprise a profit and loss account and balance sheet with auditors' and directors' reports appended. A new company's accounting reference period begins on its incorporation and runs until the following 31 March – unless the company notifies the Registrar of Companies otherwise.

   Within ten months of the end of an accounting reference period, an audited set of accounts must be laid before the shareholders at a general meeting and a set delivered to the Registrar of Companies.
10. *Registers, etc.* In addition to the accounts books, companies are required to have the following: a register of members and a share ledger; a register of directors and secretaries; a register of share transfers; a register of directors' interests in shares or debentures, etc.; a register of charges; a register of debenture holders; a book of share certificates and a minutes book. One book can be purchased to hold all the above. This will be provided automatically if you buy a ready-made company.
11. *Company seal.* All companies must also have an engraved seal. This must be impressed on share certificates and must be used whenever the company has to execute a deed. Again, this is included in the ready-made company package.

Most researchers in the United Kingdom conclude that rapid growth is more likely to be experienced by limited companies than by any of the other legal forms. One researcher, Hakim,[3] finds the same results when firms are questioned not about their actual growth, but about their plans for growth. Kalleberg and Leicht[4] and Reynolds and Miller[5] find similar results in the United States.

Cooperatives

A cooperative is an enterprise owned and controlled by the people working in it. Once in danger of becoming extinct, the workers' cooperative is enjoying something of a comeback, and there are over 1,500 operating in the United Kingdom. They are growing at the rate of 20% per annum.

Cooperatives are governed by the Industrial and Provident Societies Act 1965, whose main provisions state:

- Each member of the cooperative has equal control through the principle of 'one person, one vote'.
- Membership must be open to anyone who satisfied the stipulated qualifications.
- Profits can be retained in the business or distributed in proportion to members' involvement, e.g. hours worked.
- Members must benefit primarily from their participation in the business.
- Interest on loan or share capital is limited in some specific way, even if the profits are high enough to allow a greater payment.

It is certainly not a legal structure designed to give entrepreneurs control of their own destiny and maximum profits. However, if this is to be your chosen legal form you can pay £50 to register with the Chief Registrar of Friendly Societies, and must have at least seven members at the outset. They do not all have to be full-time workers at first. Like a limited company, a registered cooperative has limited liability (see under limited liability companies, pages 50–51) for its members and must file annual accounts, but there is no charge for this. Not all cooperatives bother to register as it is not mandatory, in which case they are treated in law as a partnership with unlimited liability.

Cooperatives are not common throughout all of the 'entrepreneurial' world, although some countries have a parallel legal structure to the UK-style cooperatives.

For example, in Denmark the AMBA is a special kind of limited company: a tax-free cooperative with its own legal regulations. The cooperative movement started at the turn of the century in the farming industry, and these cooperative companies have moved into the production of farm-related products, establishing dairies, slaughterhouses and other manufacturing units. They also include some wholesale and retail distribution channels for daily consumption goods, often officially controlled by the consumers.

The concentration of AMBAs has increased through mergers over the last fifteen years.

References

1. *Starting up in Business*, Barclays Bank Research on Small Business Characteristics, 1995.
2. Scott, M., 'Mythology and misplaced pessimism: the real failure record of small

businesses', in D. Watkins, J. Stanworth and A. Westrip (eds) *Stimulating Small Firms* (Aldershot: Gower, 1982).

3. Hakim, C., 'Identifying fast growth small firms', *Employment Gazette*, January 1989, pp. 29–41.
4. Kalleberg, A. L. and Leicht, K. T., 'Gender and organisational performance determinants of survival and small business success', *Academy of Management Journal*, **34**, 1 (1991), pp. 136–61.
5. Reynolds, P. D. and Miller, B., *Minnesota New Firms Study: An Exploration of New Firms and their Economic Contributions* (Minneapolis, MN: Centre for Urban and Regional Affairs, 1988).

4

Sources of finance

Raising money to start up a business is never easy, and expenses can vary widely from country to country. However, throughout most of the developed world there are two fundamentally different types of money which a small business can tap into. First, debt, which is money borrowed most usually from a bank, and which one day will have to be repaid. While you are making use of borrowed money you will also have to pay interest on the loan. Second, equity, which is the money either put in by shareholders, including the proprietor, and money left in the business by way of retained profit. You do not have to give the shareholders their money back, but they do expect the directors to increase the value of their shares, and if you go public they will probably expect a stream of dividends too.

If you do not meet the shareholders' expectations then they will not be there when you need more money – or if they are powerful enough, they will take steps to change the board.

Why borrowing is attractive

High gearing is the name given when the business has a high proportion of outside money to inside money. High gearing has considerable attractions to a business that wants to make high returns on shareholders' capital, as Table 4.1 shows.

In the example in Table 4.1 the business is assumed to need £60,000 capital to generate £10,000 operation profits. Four different capital structures are considered. They range from all share capital (no gearing) at one end, to nearly all loan capital at the other. The loan capital has to be 'serviced', that is, interest of 12% has to be paid. The loan itself can be relatively indefinite,

Table 4.1 The effect of gearing on ROSC

		No gearing –	Average gearing 1:1	High gearing 2:1	Very high gearing 3:1
Capital structure		£	£	£	£
Share capital		60,000	30,000	20,000	15,000
Loan capital (at 12%)		–	30,000	40,000	45,000
Total capital		60,000	60,000	60,000	60,000
Profits					
Operating profit		10,000	10,000	10,000	10,000
Less interest on loan		–	3,600	4,800	5,400
Net profit		10,000	6,400	5,200	4,600
Return on share capital	=	10,000	6,400	5,200	4,600
		60,000	30,000	20,000	15,000
	=	16.6%	21.3%	26%	30.7%
Times interest earned	=	N/A	10,000	10,000	10,000
			3,600	4,800	5,400
	=	N/A	2.3×	2.1×	1.8×

simply being replaced by another one at market interest rates when the first loan expires.

Following the table through, you can see that return on share capital (ROSC) grows from 16.6% to 30.7% by virtue of the changed gearing. If the interest on the loan were lower, the ROSC would be even more improved by high gearing, and the higher the interest, the lower the relative improvements in ROSC. So in times of low interest, businesses tend to go for increased borrowing rather than raising more equity, that is, money from shareholders.

At first sight this looks like a perpetual profit growth machine. Naturally, owners would rather have someone else 'lend' them the money for their business than put it in themselves, if they could thereby increase the return on their own investment. The problem comes if the business does not produce £10,000 operating profits. Very often, in small businesses, a drop in sales by 20% means profits have been halved or even eliminated. If profits were halved in this example, the company could not meet the interest payment on its loan. That would make the business insolvent and therefore not in a 'sound financial position' – in other words, it would be failing to meet one of the two primary business objectives.

What balance of debt to equity is right?

A company's balance gearing will be continuously changing depending on the growth opportunities that it sees ahead, the current cost of money and the availability of equity and debt capital. At certain times it is hard to raise more money from shareholders, for example when the general stock market is depressed, or if your profits performance is not up to the mark. Banks or other lenders may be your only hope. Conversely, when the conditions are right, companies frequently raise more share capital to fund growth, well in advance of needing cash.

Bankers would generally favour a 1:1 relationship between borrowed funds and share capital. But the nature of the risk involved in your business strategy is a more important factor to consider, rather than pursuing this symmetrical pair of numbers.

A more useful way to look at the debt–equity relationship is to compare money risk to business risk (see Figure 4.1).

If your business sector is generally viewed as very risky, and perhaps the most reliable measure of that risk is the proportion of firms to go bust, then financing the business almost exclusively with borrowing is tantamount to gambling.

Debt has to be serviced whatever your business performance, so it follows that in any risky, volatile marketplace, one day you stand a good chance of being caught out. Building firms are a good example of a high-risk business sector, which almost always use high-risk money. The fallacy is to believe that houses are relatively risk-free investments, and that building them is a safe enterprise too. It is no surprise that building firms top the bankruptcy rolls in both boom years and in recession. A glance at Figure 4.2 will confirm this view.

If your risks are low, the chances are that your profits are relatively low too. High profits and low risks always attract a flood of competitors, reducing your profits to levels that ultimately reflect the riskiness of your business sector. As venture capitalists and shareholders generally are looking for much better returns than they could get by lending the money, it follows that they will be disappointed in their investment on low-risk, low-returns business. So if they are wise, they will not get in in the first place, or if they do they will not put any more money in later.

With the funding matrix in mind, the small-business proprietor can begin to work towards a balance of debt and equity that is appropriate for their own business.

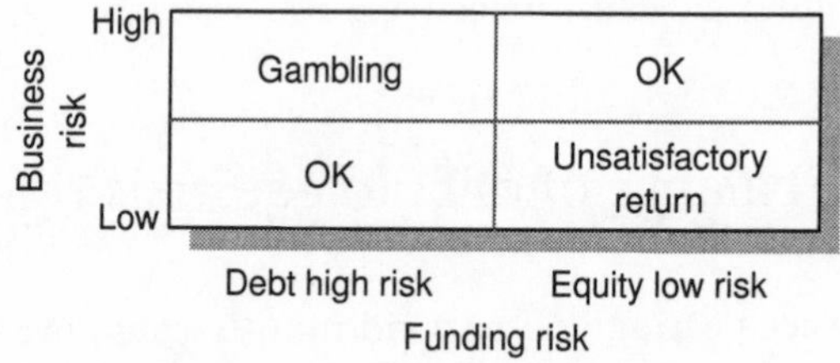

Figure 4.1 Funding matrix

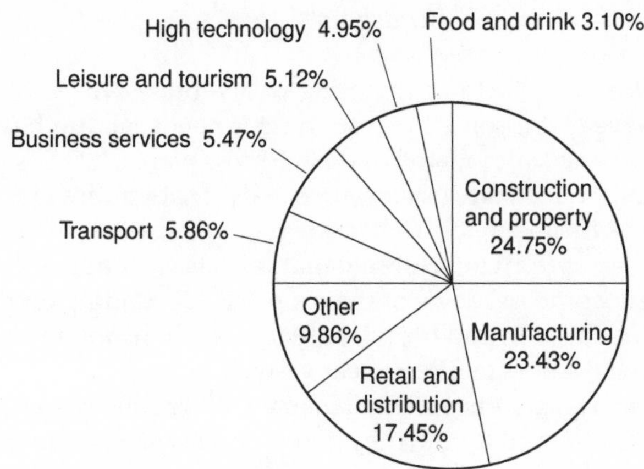

Figure 4.2 Industry analysis of receivership appointments, 1990 (source: KPWG Peat Marwick McLintock, 'Receivership Appointments in 1990').

Very often you will find it attractive to raise both sides of the equation at the same time.

What financiers look out for

Successful entrepreneurs with a proven track record can have as many problems in raising finance for their ventures as can the relative novice.

The late Bob Payton, who founded the Chicago Pizza Factory in the1970s, related a story making exactly this point, to an enterprise programme at Cranfield:

> I now have a ten-year track record in the hospitality business. My company had a turnover of £10 million this year, and made a profit of £1 million. But the one constant problem I have had for the past ten years has been raising finance to put my ideas into practice. Getting £4.5 million for my latest venture, Stapleford Park, a country house hotel in Leicestershire will, by the time it opens in May, have taken three years. It has been as difficult and as gut-wrenching as trying to raise £35,000 for my first place, the Chicago Pizza Pie Factory.
>
> Originally EMI had agreed to back my first venture. We'd shaken hands on the deal and I had ordered the ovens and gone off to the States to learn how to make pizza. When I came back I got a 'Dear John' letter. They'd decided, on reflection, not to go ahead. I have that letter still, framed and hanging on my wall in my office. After a lot of trouble I finally raised the money elsewhere and went ahead. EMI were subsequently proved to be wrong.

Financiers' needs

Anyone lending money to or investing in a venture will expect the entrepreneur to have given some thought to their needs, and to have explained how they can be accommodated in the business plan.

Bankers, and indeed any other source of debt capital, are looking for asset security to back their loan and the near certainty of getting their money back. They will also charge an interest rate that reflects current market conditions and their view of the risk level of the proposal. Depending on the nature of the business in question and the purpose for which the money is being used, bankers will take a five- to fifteen-year view.

As with a mortgage repayment, bankers will usually expect a business to start repaying both the loan and the interest on a monthly or quarterly basis as soon as the loan has been granted. In some cases a capital 'holiday' for up to two years can be negotiated, but in the early stages of any loan the interest charges make up the lion's share of payments.

Bankers hope that the business will succeed so that they can lend more money in the future and provide more banking services such as insurance, tax advice, etc., to a loyal customer.

It follows from this appreciation of the lender's needs that financiers are less interested in rapid growth and the consequent capital gain than they are in a steady stream of earning almost from the outset.

As most new or fast-growing businesses generally do not make immediate profits, money for such enterprises must come from elsewhere. Risk or equity capital, as other types of funds are called, comes from venture capital houses, as well as being put in by founders, their families and friends.

Because the inherent risks involved in investing in new and young ventures are greater than those for investing in established companies, venture capital fund managers have to offer their investors the chance of larger overall returns. To do this, fund managers must not only keep failures to a minimum, but they have to pick some big winners too – ventures with annual compound growth rates above 50%.

Example 4. 1

Debbie Moore's Pineapple dance studios was one such company. Introduced to the Unlisted Securities Market (USM) in 1982 by its venture capital providers, its shares quickly went into an 85% premium. Profits rose by 50% in 1983, as forecast, and the company raised a further £1.5 million via a rights issue. Ms Moore was given the coveted Business Woman of the Year award.

By this time the money people were not so fortunate. In 1985 aerobics began to lose its popular appeal as health experts cast doubts on its efficacy. By May the company was in a nosedive, showing half-year losses of £197,000. In the later half of 1985 Peter Bain, a new boardroom recruit, evolved a strategy to turn the company into a marketing service group. After several acquisitions and the total change of direction, Pineapple reported profits of £1.25 million in 1986.

But the dance studios clearly could not be made to work. 'It soon became obvious,' to quote Moore, 'that it was difficult to deliver the kind of money the City wanted out of dance.' Ms Moore resigned from the Pineapple Group in December 1987, taking the loss-market dance studios with her for a nominal sum, leaving the rest of the Group to pursue its new strategy.

Typically, a fund manager would expect from any ten investments: one star, seven also-rans and two flops. It is important to remember that despite this outcome, venture capital fund managers are only looking for winners, so unless you are projecting high capital growth, the chances of getting venture capital are against you.

Not only are venture capitalists looking for winners, but they are also looking for a substantial shareholding in your business. There are no simple rules for what constitutes a fair split, but *Venture Capital Report*, a UK monthly publication of investment opportunities, suggests the following starting point:

- For the idea 33%
- For the management 33%
- For the money 34%

It all comes down to how much you need the money, how risky the venture is, how much money could be made – and your skills as a negotiator. However, it is salutary to remember that 100% of nothing is still nothing. So all parties to the deal have to be satisfied if it is to succeed.

Venture capital firms may also want to put a non-executive director on the board of your company to look after their interests. You will have at your disposal a talented financial brain, so be prepared to make use of them, as their services will not be free – you will either pay up front in the fee for raising the capital, or you will pay an annual management charge.

As fast-growing companies typically have no cash available to pay dividends, investors can only profit by selling their holdings. With this in mind the venture capitalist needs to have an exit route such as the Stock Exchange or a potential corporate buyer in view at the outset.

Unlike many entrepreneurs (and some lending bankers) who see their ventures as life-long commitments to success and growth, venture capitalists have a relatively short time horizon. Typically, they are looking to liquidate small company investments within three to seven years, allowing them to pay out to individual investors and to have funds available for tomorrow's winners.

So, to be successful your business must be targeted at the needs of these two sources of finance (see Table 4.2).

Table 4.2 Financier's needs

Lenders (any safe bet)	Investors (winners only)
□ Security and low risk □ 5–15-year horizon □ Ability to pay back loan and interest immediately □ Conservative growth □ Small sums, with frequent top-ups □ No share of future profits but want a loyal long-term customer □ No management involvement	□ High risk □ But high returns □ 35% compound growth minimum □ Short time horizon 3–7 years □ But no payments until the end of the deal □ Exit route evident at outset: □ Back to founders □ Trade buyer □ USM, etc. □ Substantial shareholding: □ For the idea 33% □ For management 33% □ For money 34% □ Hands-on involvement □ Large sums, with few top-ups

Sources of funds

There are many useful directories and guides to all sources of funds for a small business.

Debt capital

There are several sources of debt capital (see Table 4.3).

The banks

As you can see from Figure 4.3, the clearing banks are the principal supplier of funds to small and growing businesses.The researchers Bannock and Doran[1] believe that bank lending to small firms is currently twice the level, in real terms, as in the 1980s. The days when you could expect to cultivate a lifetime's relationship with either a bank or a bank manager are long gone.

Banks are now into market segmentation and profit generation, so you need to be prepared to (a) shop around and (b) manage your relationship with the bank carefully.

As a rough guide, if you are with the same bank for over five years you have not pushed them hard enough. There are a myriad of things over which to negotiate with your bank, and there is a new breed of consultants who advise on banking relationships.

The bank offers the small business a wide range of services in their own

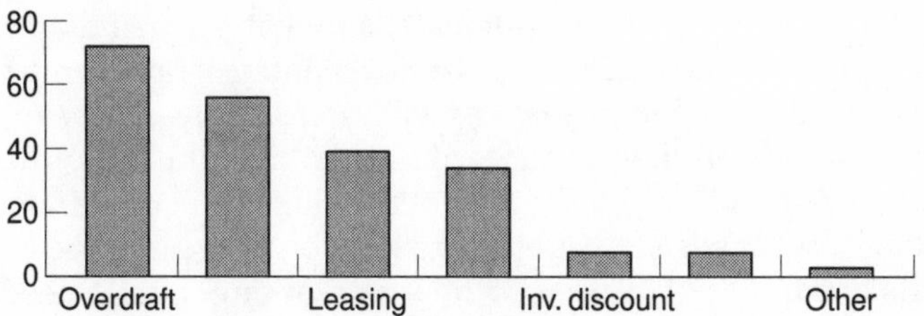

Figure 4.3 Financing small firms in the United Kingdom by percentage. (source: Kidson Impey Small Business Tracking Survey XIV, January 1995).

Table 4.3 The principal providers in the United Kingdom

Source	Usual financial range		
	Min. (£000)	Max. (£000)	Total per annum
Junior stock markets	600	3,200	300
Business Expansion Scheme:			
Private sources	5	155	70
Funds	50	2,000	40
Venture capital	50	5,000+	300
3i	10	1,000	320
Government Loan Guarantee Scheme	1	75	75
Bank lending	(at present around £20,000,000 lent)		
Local Enterprise Boards	85	100	18
Hire purchase	–	–	8,000 total
Leasing	–	–	14,000 total
Factoring	25,000+		4,000 total
Competition	0.4	30	1
Rural Development Commission	1	75	5
Tourist Boards (up to 50%)		300	–
British Overseas Trade Board	–		240
Enterprise Allowance	2		

right. Through wholly or partially owned subsidiaries they cover virtually every aspect of the financial market. These services include overdrafts, term loans, trade bill finance, factoring, leasing, export and import finance, the government loan guarantee scheme, and equity financing. Some of these services are described below. The others are explained later in this chapter.

Overdrafts

Bank overdrafts are the most common type of short-term finance.They are simple to arrange – you just talk to your local bank manager. They are flexible with no minimum level. Sums of money can be drawn or repaid within the total amount agreed. They are relatively cheap, with interest paid only on the outstanding daily balance.

Of course, interest rates can fluctuate, so what seemed a small sum of money one year can prove crippling the next if interest rates jump suddenly. Normally you do not repay the 'capital', you simply renew or alter the overdraft facility from time to time. However, overdrafts are theoretically repayable on demand, so you should not use short-term overdraft money to finance long-term needs, such as buying a lease or some plant and equipment. Overdrafts are more often used to finance working capital needs, stocks, customers who have not paid up, bulk purchases of materials and the like.

Term loans (short, medium and long)

These are rather more formal than a simple overdraft. They cover periods of 0–3, 3–10 and 10–20 years respectively. They are usually secured against an existing fixed asset or one to be acquired, or are guaranteed personally by the directors (proprietors). As such, this may involve you in a certain amount of expense with legal fees and arrangement or consultants' fees. So it may be a little more expensive than an overdraft, but unless you default on the interest charges you can be reasonably confident of having the use of the money throughout the whole term of borrowing.

The interest rates on the loan can either be fixed for the term or variable according to the prevailing interest rate. A fixed rate is to some extent a gamble which may work in your favour, depending on how interest rates move over the term of the loan; if general interest rates rise, you win; if they fall, you lose. However, a variable rate means that you do not take that risk. There is another benefit to a fixed rate of interest. Planning ahead is a little easier with a fixed financial commitment, unlike a variable overdraft rate, where a sudden rise can have disastrous consequences.

One bank has introduced a further option to alternate between fixed and variable interest rates at set time intervals, so you can learn from your mistakes! In recent years there has been a marked increase in the proportion of small firms seeking term loans rather than overdrafts.[2] Over a third of small firms have a term loan.

Government loan guarantees for small businesses

These were introduced in the United Kingdom in March 1981. The scheme was initiated in the United States and copied extensively elsewhere. Since then various Finance Acts have extended the life of the scheme by making further funds available. To be eligible for this loan, your proposition must have been looked at by an approved bank and considered viable, but should not be a proposition that the bank itself would normally support. You can be a sole trader, partnership, cooperative or limited company wanting funds to start up or expand.

The loans can be for up to £250,000 and repayable over two to seven years. It may be possible to delay paying the capital element for up to two years from the start of the loan; however, monthly or quarterly repayments of interest will have to be made from the outset. Currently 8,000 such loans are made each year in the United Kingdom.

Matched borrowing

This is a method of getting finance that matches the money against the security of a particular asset. The principal types of matched borrowing are factoring, leasing and hire purchase. Most people have explored the last two types, but for a variety of reasons many companies are highly resistant to using factoring, which is a great pity because it can often be very attractive.

Factoring and invoice discounting

In the full service, as a non-recourse factoring is known in the trade, the factoring company takes over once you have delivered your goods (or services) to the customer. All you have to do is to send the factor a duplicate invoice, and from then on they assume responsibility for your sales ledger.

The factor thus not only has the task of collecting the cash, but they also carry the can if the customer does not pay up. You can draw on up to 80% of the value of the invoice immediately, and the balance when the customer pays up – or set a number of days after the invoice has been sent out.

For this service you will pay between 0.5% and 3.5% of your turnover, and an interest charge of between 2% and 3.5% over bank base rate on any money advanced. A small setting-up charge of £500 plus will also be made, and normally a minimum level will be set on the service charge – £200 to £300 being a fairly typical base level.

Invoice discounting is the service for companies that want the cash advancing facilities offered by the factor and very little else. The service costs for invoice discounting range between 0.2% and 0.7% of turnover, much lower than for the full service. But in return you have to chase up customers for the money and assume responsibility for any bad debts.

Invoice discounting is the fastest-growing service in the factoring package, accounting for nearly 45% of all business – up from 20% in 1981.

What's in it for you?

So factoring is on the increase. Nearly 70% of all users of this type of service have turnover of less than £1 million – only 5% have turnover of more than £5 million. But exactly what benefits could it bring to a small business?

- *Helps avoid overtrading.* Unless you are in a service industry, you are lucky if your clients pay up front. The faster you get new orders, the more cash you consume. You have to pay for raw materials and labour to put products on the market before your customers pay up. If you are not careful, the eager pursuit of new business can lead to the cash flow disaster known as 'overtrading'. By factoring your debtors you can get the cash to finance growth as quickly as you can find creditworthy customers and deliver products or services to them.

- *Balancing cash requirements.* The classic source of short-term funds for a small business is an overdraft. Unfortunately, overdrafts seem to be very much a feast-or-famine affair, with facilities being increased when you do not need funds, and the supply restricted sharply when you do.

  This paradox is not caused exclusively by short-sighted bank managers – although they surely must play their part. Rather, the problem arises because the overdraft limits are usually determined by using historical balance-sheet ratios. Hence bankers are always examining the entrails for past guidance, while entrepreneurs are extolling the opportunities for the future.

  In situations of rapid growth, the banker's advice is often 'consolidate', while the factor will say 'go for it'. The factor is able to respond in this way because they are in daily or weekly contact with their client and see the flow of invoiced and payment cheques, in contrast to the banker who often works from out-of-date audited accounts, and has only a hazy recollection of what you do and for whom.

- *Improves your operating margin.* By being able to match the cash available to the level of your business activity you can get two important benefits that should have an immediate and positive effect on your operating margins.

  First, you can negotiate the finest terms from your suppliers – a luxury usually only available to those who can pay up promptly. Otherwise you have to buy what you need, wherever you can, when you can afford it – not a recipe for great economy.

  Second, with a predictable cash flow, you can plan production schedules and stock-holding in a manufacturing business, to optimize plant efficiencies. This is in sharp contrast to those whose cash shortages force them to move labour and materials around in a haphazard way which inevitably results in more down-time, higher unit labour costs and more material wastage.

- *You can concentrate on what you do best – running the business.* Once you start to view your customers simply as debtors, your marketing focus will become blurred. In any event, the chances are that you are better at making and selling than you are at playing policemen chasing up late payers. Factoring allows you to concentrate on what you do best, and leaves them to their field – collecting cash.

  We know of one company that used to take ninety days to collect money from customers. This is now down to fifty on average a year after introducing factoring. It also leaves your sales people's relationships with customers intact, rather than damaged through constant pestering for payment. They can also spend more time on selling, which should pay handsome dividends. If this does not happen, look carefully at exactly what your sales people are doing.

- *You can trim overheads.* Not only can factoring allow you to spend more time managing the business rather than the sales ledger, you can save the overhead cost currently incurred in running your own credit control department. One company we know gets a factoring service for £12,000 per annum, less than the cost of employing a credit controller and finding a desk for them to sit at!

  Factoring will also allow you to optimize the resources needed to collect cash, rather than using the blitz approach that is common to so many small firms. In other words, the effort put into cash collection is always maintained in proportion to the amount of cash to be collected – a feat near impossible to attain when you run your own credit control. The chances are that you will get a more professional service into the bargain when it comes to such matters as assessing credit risk and insuring against bad debts. Factoring is a source of off-balance-sheet finance. Under current accounting conventions it is not necessary to reveal how much of the business's funds have been made available from factoring. This means that key balance-sheet ratios such as gearing and return on capital employed will be influenced in favour of companies using factoring. Suppose, for example, your present financial structure involved using £100,000 of share capital and reserves, and £100,000 of bank loans: your 'gearing' would be 50%.

  If you need a further £100,000 to finance growth and you borrow it from the bank, your gearing would increase to 67%. This would make your business look more risky to any observer, such as a potential supplier, customer or new shareholder. If the extra funds came from factoring your debtors, you could finance the growth – and your gearing ratio would remain unchanged at 50%.

  The same argument holds for the return on capital employed (ROCE) ratio. The higher you make the sum of capital, reserves and loans, the lower the ratio will be for any given level of profit. Once again, the lower your ROCE, the worse your business appears to be performing in the eyes of the financial world.

  Of course, loan capital is not the only type of money available to the growing firm. You could raise more share capital – but this route can be expensive, time-consuming and it will dilute your stake in the business. All in all, there will be occasions when factoring is infinitely preferable to taking on board new shareholders.

Leasing companies

Leasing is a way of getting the use of vehicles, plant and equipment without paying the full cost all at once. Operating leases are taken out where you will use the equipment for less than its full economic life – for example, a car, photocopier or vending machine. The lessor takes the risk of the equipment becoming obsolete, and assumes responsibility for repairs, maintenance and insurance. As you, the lessee, are paying for this service, it is more expensive than a finance lease, where you lease the equipment for most of its economic life and maintain and insure it yourself. Leases can normally be extended, often for fairly nominal sums, in the later years.

The obvious attractions of leasing are that no deposit is needed, leaving your working capital for more profitable use elsewhere. Also, the cost of leasing is known from the start, making forward planning simpler. There may even be some tax advantages over other forms of finance.

Leasing companies may be a little more adventurous in dealing with new and small businesses than other sources of finance.

Most leasing companies are subsidiaries of much larger financial institutions, including the clearing banks. Some of them operate in specialist markets such as aircraft or agricultural, as their names imply. Many would not look at anything under £1 million.

Finance houses (hire purchase)

These provide instalment credit for short-term needs such as hire purchase. Hire purchase differs from leasing in that you have the option at the start to become the owner of the equipment after a series of payments have been made. The interest is usually fixed and often more expensive than a bank loan. However, manufacturers (notably car makers) often subsidize this interest, so it pays to shop around both for sources of hire purchase finance and manufacturers of equipment.

Hire purchase is now used to finance the purchase of most types of business asset. Sixty of the 100 largest UK enterprises and 45% of all small firms are regular users of hire purchase facilities.

Shareholders' funds (equity)

There are three principal vehicles for attracting new investors to help finance a small business.

Business angels

For small sums of money, from a few thousand pounds upwards, you could contact a business angel. An angel is a private individual who is willing to put their money and perhaps their efforts into your business. This informal venture capital sector has been most investigated in the United States. Two researchers, Gaston[3] and Wetzel,[4] estimated that business angels provide between two and five times the funds that the established venture capital providers do. The authoritative research in the United Kingdom[5] estimates the informal risk capital pool to be between £2 billion and £4 billion. The median investment range for business angels is £10,000–£30,000.[6] Not only will angels put in smaller sums of money than conventional venture capital providers, but they are more prepared to back start-ups and riskier projects – if the chemistry is right. To contact an angel you will probably have to use an introductory agency such as LINC (Local Investment Networking Company), which circulate to subscribing investors a regular bulletin of abbreviated information on business projects. LINC also helps those seeking finance to put together a business plan and a summary of their investment proposal. There are now more than a score of regional angels networks under the LINC banner. For more details contact: LINC, 4 Snow Hill, London EC1A 2BS (tel. 0171–236 3000). The whole angels sector was given a boost in the 1993 budget with the introduction of the Enterprise Investment Scheme (EIS). The key features of the scheme are:

- up-front tax relief at 20% for investors
- no tax on capital gains income and capital gains tax relief on losses
- annual investment of up to £100,000
- companies may raise up to £1 million a year
- investors may become paid directors.

Venture capital providers

Over fifty providers of venture capital are members of the British Venture Capital Association (BVCA). The BVCA was formed in 1983 to help further the provision of such financing in the United Kingdom. Venture capital of around £1.65 billion is invested in over 1,000 firms in the United Kingdom each year. Only in the United States is there a greater provision of venture capital. The largest player in this market is 3Is (Investors in Industry), formed in 1945, which accounts for around half of all this type of investment, with stakes in over 5,000 businesses. It is the only UK venture capital provider with a regional network, and the only one in Europe with offices in most of the important cities. The British Venture Capital Association and the accountants KPMG Peat Marwick, among others, maintain a comprehensive database of venture capital sources. Table 4.4 shows where venture capitalists put their money in terms of the stage of the business.

Table 4.4 Venture financing by stage of business

Stage	%
Pre start-up	10
Start-up	25
Early stage development	28
Late stage development	26
Management buy-out	11
Total	100

Venture capital providers fall into two camps: those who think they can add value to a business by giving hands-on help and advice, as well as investing money, and those who leave well alone. There is no evidence in Europe[7] or in the United States[8] that there is any difference in the performance of investee companies whether a 'hands on' or 'hands off' approach is taken. There is plenty of anecdotal evidence that one reason entrepreneurs shy away from venture capital is the fear that they will have their decisions interfered with.

Going public

There are two possible stock markets in the United Kingdom on which to gain a public listing. This structure is used in the United States and France and now is gradually being adopted elsewhere. A full Stock Exchange listing calls for profits of at least £1 million and usually much more. At least 25% of the company's shares must be put up for sale and there should be at least 200 shareholders after the listing. Entrepreneurs rarely go this route too early. In the first instance, as they expect their businesses to become very successful they are loath to 'give away' so much of the equity at a bargain-basement price. Second, few entrepreneurs enjoy either the public scrutiny that comes with a stock market listing, or the real threat of being taken over. The Alternative Investment Market (AIM) is much more attractive for entrepreneurs seeking equity capital. Formed in 1995 to replace the Third Market and the Unlisted Securities Market (USM), AIM provides risk capital for new rather than established ventures. It has an altogether more relaxed atmosphere. AIM now has around 200 companies whose shares are traded on the market and its own index, the FTSE AIM index. The formalities for getting onto AIM really are minimal. A prospectus, which must contain all the information that an investor could reasonably require to make an informed assessment of the business and its prospects, has to be prepared. But a nominated adviser such as Ernst & Young, Casenove, Charterhouse or one of another fifty or so major institutions is on hand to steer you through the application process. You have to have such an adviser to get onto AIM, as well as a broker who has agreed in advance to make a market in your shares. Such advisers can also act as a sort of quality control, ensuring that new AIM entrants have at least the makings of a profitable venture. Once on the AIM market a successful company and its founders will have access to a continuous stream of new risk-free finance from a wide base of investors to underwrite their growth. This will be preferable to relying on either bank borrowings or a single venture capital provider for what may well be the riskiest stage in their corporate life – the growth phase. On average in the first year each AIM company experiences 570 share transactions averaging £9,000, so, unlike unquoted private companies, those on AIM are able to put an accurate value on the business. The AIM market should also prove a good preparation for companies wanting to go for a full quote later on, or for entrepreneurs who are planning their exit route. The bad news is that AIM is not a cheap source of funds. The less you raise, the more expensive it can be. Omnicare, a distributor of oxygen therapy equipment, raised £400,000 at a cost of £127,000, or about a third of the money raised. The average cost of an AIM float is just under 7% – about the same as joining the main stock market. A company seeking between £5 million and £10 million could end up paying between £350,000 and £600,000 to get onto AIM. Going the venture capital route could cost as little as £250,000. But with venture capital you end up with one shareholder who is more likely to want an exit than to put in more money to help you grow.

A flotation on either of these markets is a major project and proprietors would be well advised to plan some three years ahead to ensure that the company is in the best possible shape when it comes to market.

The objective must be to present a sound profit record and balance sheet, along with further growth, which will make the company attractive to investors.

As you draw up your flotation plan and timetable, you should have the following matters in mind, according to accountants Touche Ross:

- *Advisers.* You will need to be supported by a team which will include a sponsor, stockbroker, reporting accountant and solicitor. These should be respected firms, active in flotation work and familiar with the company's type of business. You and your company may be judged by the company you keep, so choose advisers of good repute and make sure that the personalities work effectively together. It is very unlikely that a small local firm of accountants, however satisfactory, will be up to this task.
- *Sponsor.* You will need to appoint a financial institution, usually a merchant banker, to fill this important role. If you do not already have a merchant bank in mind, your accountant will offer guidance. The job of the sponsor is to coordinate and drive the project forward.
- *Timetable.* It is essential to have a timetable for the final months during the run-up to a float – and to adhere to it. The company's directors and senior staff will be fully occupied in providing information and attending meetings. They will have to delegate and there must be sufficient back-up support to ensure that the business does not suffer.
- *Management team.* A potential investor will want to be satisfied that your company is well managed: at board level and below. It is important to ensure succession, perhaps by offering key directors and managers service agreements and share options. It is wise to draw on the experience of well-qualified non-executive directors.
- *Accounts.* The objective is to have a profit record that is rising but, in achieving this, you will need to take into account directors' remuneration and pension contributions and to eliminate any expenditure that might be

acceptable in a privately owned company but that would not be acceptable in a public company, namely excessive perks such as yachts, luxury cars, lavish expense accounts and holiday homes.

Accounts must be consolidated and audited to appropriate accounting standards and the audit reports must not contain any major qualifications. The auditors will need to be satisfied that there are proper stock records and a consistent basis of valuing stock during the years prior to flotation. Accounts for the last three years (two years in respect of the USM) will need to be disclosed and the date of the last accounts must be within six months (nine months for the USM) of the issue.

The rewards

In the first nine years of the USM's existence over 500 entrepreneurs have been made millionaires. The USM millionaires include John Aspinall, the Kent zoo-keeper, and the late Sir James Goldsmith. They shared £48 million in equal halves when the Aspinall Casino Group was floated. Though still in its infancy, the AIM market looks like delivering similar value to entrepreneurs. In fact, going public is about the only way that you can become seriously rich in business and stay in control of your company. With venture capital you are always susceptible to the pressures of the capital providers. They want an exit route so that they can plough their clients' funds into new and 'even more exciting ventures', so if the opportunity for a trade sale comes along, the chances are that they will sell you to the highest bidder. This may make you rich, but it is unlikely to make you seriously rich and it will certainly leave you in the passenger seat rather than the driver's.

Banks, as we have already discussed, are largely fair-weather friends, and you certainly will not get rich borrowing more from them.

Going public also puts the stamp of respectability on you and your company. It will enhance the status and credibility of your business, and it will enable you to borrow against the 'security' provided by your new shareholders, should you so wish. Your shares will also provide an attractive way to retain and motivate key staff. By giving, or rather allowing them to earn, share options at discounted prices, they too can participate in the capital gains that you are making.

With a public share listing you can now join in the take-over and asset-stripping game. When your share price is high and things are going well, you can look out for weaker firms to gobble up – and all you have to do is offer them more of your shares in return for theirs. You do not even have to find real money. But of course this is a two-sided game and you yourself may now become the target of a hostile bid.

The penalties

So much for the rewards – the penalties are equally awesome, and they can happen before you even get a listing, as described in the story below.

Example 4.2

Kevin McNeany, founder and managing director of Nord Anglia Education, spent four months and £300,000 preparing his company for a flotation on the Unlisted Securities Market (USM). Last December, on the day before the price of issue was due to be announced, McNeany decided that his company, which runs sixteen private schools and five language schools, was being valued too cheaply and cancelled the flotation.

'I wasn't willing to accept the price because it was 20% less than what had been suggested before,' says McNeany, a former teacher who, over the past eighteen years, has built up a company with turnover of £8.2 million and pre-tax profits of £610,000.

'My financial advisers said, "You cannot do this." I said, "I am,"' recalls McNeany. Disappointed, despondent and £300,000 poorer, McNeany took the train back to Manchester from London to re-negotiate credit lines with his bankers which he had thought the flotation would render unnecessary.

The next penalty is that public companies come under the greater scrutiny of a larger and more perceptive investment community. For example, Spice, the motor parts distributor which has just gone into receivership, was scuppered in its first attempt to join the USM when the Stock Exchange found that the financial controller had been convicted of fraud. Another company that came unstuck after its flotation was Sharp & Law, a shop-fitter, which joined the Unlisted Securities Market in 1987. Two years later, it discovered errors in 1987 figures when payment for some large contracts had been double-counted. Arthur Young, the accountants, who were called in to investigate, produced a report calling for improvements to the company's senior financial management, the appointment of a managing director and an organizational systems and computer department review. The company never recovered, however, and went into receivership last year.

You may also find that being in the public eye not only cramps your style but fills up your engagement diary too. Most entrepreneurs find that they have to spend up to a quarter of their time in the City, explaining their strategies, in the months preceding and the first years following their going public. It is not unusual for so much management time to have been devoted to answering accountants' and stockbrokers' questions that there is not enough time to run the day-to-day business, and profits drop as a direct consequence.

The City also creates its own 'pressure' both to seduce companies onto the market and then require them to perform beyond any reasonable expectations. For example, Michael Aukett, chief executive of Aukett, the architectural practice, is less sure that he would not consider his options if he had his time again. Aukett went public in February 1988 and maintained its steady promise in June this year by turning in highly respectable interims. Profits shot up 20% to £947,000.

Yet Mr Aukett says: 'The City is responsible for creating the hype and that any size of business should go on the market, but architectural firms are basically too small. We do not begin to command any position under a market capitalization of £50 million.'

With the benefit of hindsight, Mr Aukett believes now that he should have waited another three years to grow to a bigger size before tangling with the institutions: 'They seduce you to go in and when the market goes on its knees, they do not support you. How do our share-holding staff feel when they see the market dip?'

One final penalty worth mentioning is the apparent lack of a direct relationship between the business's profit performance and its share price. Confidence, rumour and the sentiment for certain business sectors which fall in and out of favour, all play a part in moving share prices up and down – and at the end of the day that's all public shareholders and City institutions care about. Polly Peck is a fairly vivid example of this problem. The auditors' report dated 17 April 1990 showed that the company had made £161 million profit and the share price stood at 417p, making the company worth £2 billion, on paper. By 20 September the company's shares were suspended at 108p on the back of rumours about alleged share-dealing irregularities. A month later the company went into administrative receivership and the shares were declared worthless.

Whatever the downside risk on going public, it is as well to remember that several thousand private companies go bust for every public company that goes under. In the long run, the only realistic way to get big, very rich and survive is to go public.

Other ways to fund a small business

Industry backers

Example 4.3

Safetynet is a company that specializes in providing back-up computer services for companies whose computer systems are put out of action in the short term by fire, flood or even human error.

The company was set up five years ago by two former IBM salesmen, and it now has 230 subscribers, of whom only 19 ever experienced a 'disaster'. The company's turnover is £3 million and pre-tax profits are around £1 million. Their seventeen competitors are not doing quite so well, as none make any money, according to Safetynet's founders.

Compatibility being all-important in the computer business, Safetynet has had to specialize. It is only interested in disasters affecting the medium-range IBM machines. The decision to concentrate on this area appears to have been influenced by the knowledge that IBM's AS 400 was going to prove a highly popular machine. There are at least 500 of them in the City now.

Convinced that they had hit upon a sound proposition, they then had to convince others. Venture capitalists were not enthusiastic but another approach proved more rewarding.

Reasoning that their prime requirement would be equipment, they approached companies in the industry for support. Eventually, United Computers provided hardware in exchange for a 14% stake. Bluebird Software, now IBM's largest agency in the mid-range but then a relatively new company which had bought its first computer from Paul Hearson, agreed to cover all the business's variable costs, and took a 26% stake.

As Safetynet has grown, the founders have been able to buy out their early backers for more than £600,000.

The two founders are now the sole owners of the company and seem happy to keep it that way. Talk of a flotation has stopped. 'We feel very cool about going public,' says Paul Hearson.

Franchising

This too is a popular method of financing the growth of a small firm. It is covered in Chapter 6.

References

1. Bannock, G. and Doran, A., *Venture Capital and the Equity Gap* (London: National Westminster Bank, 1991).
2. Binks, M. R., Ennew, C. T. and Reed, G. V., *Small Business and their Banks*, (Knutsworth: Forum of Private Business, 1992).
3. Gaston, R. J., 'The scale of informal capital markets', *Small Business Economics*, **1**, 3, 1989, pp. 223–30.
4. Wetzel, W. E. Jr., 'The informal venture capital market: aspects of scale and market efficiency', *Journal of Business Venturing*, **2**, 1987, pp. 229–313.
5. Harrison, R. T. and Mason, C. M., 'Finance for the growing business: the role of informal investment', *National Westminster Bank Review*, May 1993, pp. 17–29.
6. Mason, C. M., Harrison, R. T. and Chaloner, J., *Informal Risk Capital in the UK: A Study of Investor Characteristics, Investment Preferences and Investment Decision Making*, Venture Finance Research Project Working Paper No. 2, University of Southampton, 1991.
7. Fredriksen, O., Olofsson, C. and Wahlbin, C., 'The role of venture capital in the development of portfolio companies', paper for the SMS Conference: Strategic Bridging, Stockholm, September 1990.
8. MacMillan, I. C., Kulow, G. M. and Choylian, R., 'Venture capitalists' involvement in their investments: extent and performance', *Journal of Business Venturing*, **4**, 1 (1989), pp. 27–47.

5

Start-up strategies

The business idea and how a small business can exploit it

At the outset of every small business venture lies the founders' belief either that they have recognized an opportunity unnoticed by others, or that they can do something better, i.e. as in a more innovative manner than the existing suppliers.

One of the sad aspects of the high failure rate for new businesses in the first year or so of life is that often that failure involved someone investing a lump-sum payment received from a redundancy. It is one of the paradoxes of small business that whereas you cannot start without investing some time and money, it may be safer to have more time than money. Those with money, from whatever source, frequently have less pressure on them from banks or financial investors to research their ideas thoroughly first, simply because they do not have to go to see the bank manager in the early stages, to obtain support before starting. Those with time but inadequate resources always do have to seek advice before starting, and inevitably this will include researching the market as widely as possible before commencing. You do not have to open a shop to prove that there are no customers for your goods or services; frequently, some modest 'DIY' market research beforehand can give clear guidance as to whether your venture will succeed or not.

This chapter reviews the principal ways in which a business idea can be 'born' and exploited.

The ways in

So much for the general approach applied by entrepreneurs to validate their business idea. There are two fundamentally different ways of exploiting a business idea: starting up on your own in your own style; or taking on someone else's business or style of operation.

Both approaches have variations and pros and cons.

Starting up from scratch

The most common reasons for wanting to start up a business from scratch usually lie in the direct personal experiences of the business founder(s). Some common examples include the following:

Spotting a gap in the market

This involves taking a business concept that works well in other places and finding a new and undersupplied or undercompeted market in which to set up. In practice this is probably the most common way into business.

The chances of success when starting up in this way are greatly improved when the founder knows and understands the markets and products/services involved. After that, location is the key.

Example 5.1

Chantal Coady, who founded Rococo, the King's Road 'designer' chocolate and confectionery business, recognized that location was crucial to the success or failure of her business. Her shop is sited at the World's End section of the King's Road, Chelsea, at the junction of Beaufort Street. This is conveniently located for the Chelsea/Knightsbridge clientele. There is a good passing trade and a generally creative ambience on this road, and no other specialist chocolate shop in the vicinity. World's End was not chosen on a whim; it was the subject of a most careful study. While Chantal was confident that her 'Rococo' concept was unique, she was enough of a realist to recognize that at one level it could be seen as just another upmarket chocolate shop. As such, her shop needed its own distinctive catchment area. She drew up a map of chocolate shops situated in Central London which verified her closest competitors to be in Knightsbridge – in central London terms, another world. In short, she had found a gap in the market.

A further subject of concern was the nature of the passing trade in the vicinity of the proposed World's End shop. The local residents could be polled by direct leafleting, but she decided to find out more about the passing trade by means of a questionnaire, which responded favourably to the Rococo concept.

Inventions and inventors

Inventions and inventors fall into the 'starting up from scratch' category of small business venture. While it is true that small firms are more effective than large ones at coming up with innovative ideas (see Chapter 2), it is also true that most 'brilliant' new ideas do not make good business.

Geoffrey Timmons, Professor of Entrepreneurial Studies at North-eastern University, has coined the phrase 'better mousetrap fallacy' to describe the often unwarranted faith put into a new product or invention by entrepreneurs, especially if it has been granted a patent. His thesis is that technological ideas must indeed be sound, but that marketability and marketing know-how generally outweigh technical elegance in the success equation. To illustrate this claim, Professor Timmons' research shows that less than 0.5% of the best ideas contained in the *US Patent Gazette* in the last five years have returned a dime to the inventors.

Many previous studies (Rothwell *et al.*,[1] Von Hippel,[2] and Madique and Zirger[3]) have confirmed that, while innovation is a vital ingredient in business success, unless:

- there are clear market signals showing a need for the innovation
- the product or service has been specified by customers
- the innovators work closely with customers as the product or service is being developed

then the chances of the innovation or invention being accepted quickly into the market are low. The important word here is 'quickly'. Most inventor-based start-ups do not have the funds to wait years for customers to get used to their new idea.

New business opportunities

Sometimes completely new business opportunities are created. These can be brought about by economic factors, technological development, changes in the way that people work and live or a subtle combination of many factors.

The skill for the small business founder lies in both recognizing that the opportunity is about to occur, and when and how it should be exploited.

Examples here include such businesses as video rentals and cottage rental agencies. In the case of the former, without the ready availability of films at a high selling price, a relatively high market penetration by video players and a growth in the appreciation of home entertainments, no business opportunity could exist for video hire shops.

Even with a strong market demand, the relatively low cost of entry and the lack of any specialist skill required by video shop-owners caused the market to be grossly oversupplied almost from the outset. A general recession swept away large numbers of these new entrants, and now the market is in the hands of a new generation of more professional 'retailers'.

The cottage rental business has emerged in Europe with the advent of increased affluence and leisure time, second homes becoming fashionable, and farming communities shrinking as a result of their improved efficiency.

These factors, combined with a healthy tax break for those letting out their properties, have created an opportunity for businesses to set up and meet the needs of holiday-makers with properties to let.

One UK company, Country Holidays, set up in the late 1970s, at the early stage of this market, was sold a decade later for £14 million.

Back in 1967 Peter Fraiman discovered that there was a virtually brand-new market in the United Kingdom for refurbished electronic equipment. He financed Electronic Brokers from his savings of £3,000 and a £1,500 bank loan, and initially ran it from his home. Twenty years later sales had topped the £5 million mark.

Other people's failures

Very often the small business founder's imagination will have been fired by the frustration of receiving inferior or inadequate satisfaction from an existing product or service. Out of this opportunity a new business is created.

Example 5.2

Tom Farmer, the son of a Leith shipping clerk who earned £5 a week, launched Kwik-Fit in 1971. By 1990 the company had a turnover of £200 million, made £40 million profit and employed 3,400 people by servicing 3.5 million cars a year. Farmer founded the business out of a deep dissatisfaction with the level of service provided by garage servicing. No one ever called customers to tell them when their cars were ready, and the bills bore no relation to the original estimates. In his own words, the enduring philosophy behind his business, to which he ascribes its success, is: '100% customer satisfaction. Just giving service – phoning back in half-an-hour if you say you will, standing by promises – puts you miles ahead of anyone else in the field.'

Shirt Point, started just before Christmas 1987, is the brain-child of ad-man Robert Barclay and his friend since primary school, art dealer Jeremy Wayne. 'We were having lunch eighteen months ago and complaining about the hassle we had trying to get shirts done,' says Barclay, aged 29. 'High performers in the City, earning perhaps £100,000 a year and working from 7 a.m. until 7 p.m., still have to get up at the crack of dawn to iron a shirt.'

Their catchment area was initially restricted to the City and they laundered up to 1,000 shirts a week, charging £3.65 a piece. Hard-pressed brokers and bankers could take their dirty laundry to the office, telephone Shirt Point, have it collected the same day and then returned, hand-finished with buttons sewn on and collars renewed where necessary, within forty-eight hours. This proved more attractive than the 'same day' service offered by dry cleaner shops.

Buying an existing business

Buying out an existing business on a friendly basis has a number of advantages over starting up a small business from scratch. The basic business idea still needs to be validated by market research.

In the 1990s on average each year in the United Kingdom some 2,000 private companies changed hands, valued at £19 billion. The average size, in turnover terms, of the companies bought and sold was under £5 million per annum, with many having sales below £0.5 million.

Of these acquisitions 45% were viewed as wholly amicable; there was a willing buyer and a willing seller, and no other parties were involved. Another 45% were classified either as having several interested buyers, or there was resistance from the vendor to being taken over. Only 10% of the acquisitions were hostile, with a bid being made over the heads of the vendor's board.

These contested bids are the only deals that make the headlines. But, as you can see, the reality is that an awful lot of quite small companies are changing hands in a fairly friendly way, for modest sums of money.

When economic growth is virtually static, or if you want to achieve really dramatic growth, then buying someone else's business can be a very attractive option. But, be warned: while 90% of acquisitions took place under friendly conditions, only 55% were eventually rated as successful or very successful by both buyers and sellers (see Table 5.1). So buying a company is certainly not always a sure-fire winning strategy.

Why do you want to buy?

If you are buying a company to expand your business you need to think your reasons through carefully. Big companies end up on the take-over trail because of management ego, or corporate strategy. Over 40% of big companies listed 'sending signals to the City' as their principal reason for buying. A further 35% put it down to 'the chairman's insistence'. For smaller companies the reasons to buy need to be rather more practical. Sound reasons for acquisitions include the following:

- To increase market share and eliminate a troublesome competitor.
- To broaden product range or give access to new markets.
- To diversify into new markets, acquiring the necessary management, marketing or technical skills to enable you to capture a reasonable slice of the market, relatively quickly.
- To get into another country or region.
- To protect an important source of supply which could be under threat from a competitor.
- To acquire additional staff, factory space, warehousing, distribution channels, or to get access to additional major customers more quickly than by starting up yourself.

You should produce a written statement explaining the rationale behind your reason to buy before you start looking for possible companies, otherwise

Table 5.1 Buyers' and sellers' assessment of the results of the acquisition

	%
Very successful	20
Successful	35
So-so	20
Unsuccessful	17
Very unsuccessful	8

you end up pursuing a 'bargain' just because it seems cheap, although it has absolutely nothing to do with your previously defined commercial goals.

It is also worth remembering that companies available at knock-down prices are likely to need drastic surgery. So unless you fancy yourself as a company doctor, stay well away.

What do you want to buy?

It takes a year of work, on average, to find and buy a private limited company. The more accurately you describe your ideal purchase, the simpler, quicker and cheaper your search will be.

Just imagine trying to buy a house without any idea of where you wanted to live, how much you wanted to spend, how many bedrooms were needed, whether you wanted a new house or a listed building, or if you wanted a garden. The search would be near impossible to organize, it could take forever and the resulting purchase would almost certainly please no one.

The same problem is present when buying a company. The definition of what you want to buy should explain the following:

- ☐ The business area, products/service the company is in.
- ☐ The location.
- ☐ The price range and the cash you have available.
- ☐ The management depth and the management style you are looking for.
- ☐ The minimum profitability and return on capital employed that you could accept. It is worth remembering that if the company you plan to buy only makes 1% profit while you make 5%, and you are of equal size, the resultant profit will be 3% [(5 + 1) ÷ 2].
- ☐ The image compatibility between your company and the target company.
- ☐ Scope for integration and cost savings.
- ☐ The tax status.

Outside the factors listed above you may have vital reasons which, if not achieved, would make the acquisition a poor bet. For example, if you want to iron out major cash flow or plant capacity cycles, there is little point in going for a business similar to your own; it will only make the peaks and troughs more pronounced.

Start searching

Once you have a profile of the sort of company to buy, you can begin to assemble your shopping list.

You have the following possible routes to find a business to buy:

- Business pages in quality papers and magazines are increasingly devoting sections to lists of companies for sale. *The Economist* has joined this growing band of media offering a service to buyers and sellers of private companies.
- Accountants and lawyers frequently produce lists of private companies for sale. You can always circulate your shopping list to them. This activity is not just confined to the top eight firms. Most sizeable practices will be in this market.
- Venture capitalists looking for exit routes will also have companies for sale.
- There are also specialist companies in the mergers and acquisitions field which exist solely to bring buyers and sellers together. They usually operate on a 'no-deal, no-fee basis'.

Investigate and approach

Once you have drawn up your shopping list, arm yourself with everything you can find out about prospective purchases. Get their literature, get samples, copies of their advertising, any press comment and, of course, their accounts. Then go out and take a look at their premises and as much of their operation as it is possible to see. If you cannot get in, can you send one of your sales people to suss things out? This investigation will help you to both shorten your shopping list and put it in order of priority. Now you are ready for the approach.

Although you are technically 'buying', psychologically you would be well advised to think of acquiring a company as a selling job. As such you cannot afford to have any approach rejected either too early or without a determined effort.

You have three options as to how to make the initial approach and each has its merits. You can telephone, giving only the broadest reason for your call – saying perhaps that you wish to discuss areas of common interest. You could write and be a little more specific about your purpose, following that with a telephone call to arrange a meeting, perhaps over lunch. Finally, you could use a third party such as an accountant, merchant bank or consultant. Reasons of secrecy could make this method desirable, and if executive time is at a premium there may be no other practicable way.

The first meeting is crucial and you need to achieve two objectives. First, you must establish mutual respect, trust and rapport. Nothing worthwhile will follow without these. Then you need to establish in principle that both parties are seriously interested. The time-scale, price, methods of integration, etc., can all be side-stepped until later, except in the most general sense.

Any investigation should focus on very specific questions. The list of questions and suggestions for finding the answers should include the following:

- □ What has been the trend of profits for the firm over the last five years or so? To find the answer:

  (a) ask for copies of audit accounts

  (b) review the firm's books

  (c) study copies of bank deposits for the period

  (d) study copies of income tax returns for the past five years.

  If the seller will not provide these items, the buyer should doubt the claimed profitability.
- □ Is the business growing, declining, or relatively stable? The prime measure here is sales volume. Authenticity of sales claims should be verified, especially if the company for sale is a subsidiary of another firm.
- □ Are profits and profit margins consistent with sales volume?
- □ Why does the present owner wish to sell? There may be entirely legitimate reasons for the decision, such as health, age or a desire to move.
- □ Does the balance sheet for the firm reflect a sound current financial condition? Are the debtors current or a collection of well-overdue accounts? Is the stock fresh, modern merchandise, or does it include much obsolete merchandise which will be hard to sell?
- □ Are the fixed assets properly valued? Are they in good condition?
- □ Are expenses in line with average statistics for this type of firm? The answer here is to refer to comparative statistics while recognizing that there may be reasons for variations in the particular case.
- □ If the premises are rented, what is the nature of the lease? Can it be renewed? For what periods of time? What conditions are attached to rent reviews?
- □ What is the competition in the area? By buying instead of setting up a new firm, one competitor has been eliminated. However, the nature of remaining competition is still important.
- □ What are the present owner's plans after the sale? Too often new buyers find that the seller is in competition with them soon after the sale. The best assurance against this is a clause in the sales agreement restricting such action.
- □ Are the present employees satisfactory?
- □ What are the prospects for increasing profits? Even though the business has been profitable in the past, the competent buyer will analyze the floor space, the layout, the lines of goods carried, the market area and the

services now rendered in terms of whether or not a greater volume of sales and profits would be possible.

- □ What is the customer and neighbourhood attitude towards the firm?
- □ What is the reputation of the firm among business people in the area?
- □ Do suppliers regard the seller favourably?
- □ Is the community that the firm will serve a growing one?
- □ Are all liabilities correctly stated on the balance sheet? Individual contracts and other obligations may be checked in detail. The best protection for the new buyer is a clause in the sales agreement providing that any other claims or liabilities are those of the seller. Purchase of the specific assets and stated claims by a separate legal entity may be appropriate.
- □ Would the investment make as high a return as could be made by starting a new firm? The answer to the question will set an upper limit to price negotiation.

Valuing the business

Once you have found a business that you want to buy, and that is probably for sale, you will now need your accountants to investigate the business in depth to see exactly what is on offer. This can take several weeks, and it is a little like having a house surveyed. You need to remember that normally accounts are prepared on the 'going concern basis', which implies that the company is going to continue trading much as before. This means that the historical cost of fixed assets such as buildings, land, machinery, etc., can appear in the balance sheet, rather than the market worth. After all, until you came along they had not planned to sell their fixed assets, but now the figures will have to be re-cast using different principles.

Ultimately, what you are buying is either extra profit, or perhaps lower costs in your own business. You have to decide how much that is worth. Public companies usually have rules of thumb for each sector. So, for example, much of the retail sector is valued on a p/e of 12, which means retailers are seen as being worth twelve times last year's net profit. A private company in the same sector would only be worth two-thirds of that figure, as their shares are less easily bought and sold. The worth of the assets in the business would also be important, and whatever the business it is usually people and their knowledge and skills that you are buying – unless of course you are simply asset stripping.

Prices paid for private companies are monitored in a new three-monthly index prepared by the accountancy firm, Stoy Hayward. The index is published in the magazine *Acquisitions Monthly* and will enable owners of private companies to follow trends in unquoted company acquisitions and help them to assess a fair price for their own businesses.

Based on completed acquisitions, it will track the ratio between the purchase price of private companies sold during a three-month period and their historic earnings.

The price/earnings ratio of the index stood at 9.8 during the first quarter of 1990, nearly 20% lower than the trading p/e multiple of companies in the FT 500 Index for the same period.

There is no great science in valuing business, just a rather messy art – and at the end of the day you can always work out if it would be cheaper to start up from scratch yourself. That will give you an outer figure for your negotiations.

Limit the risks

Buying a business will always be risky. If you have done your homework and got the price right, with any luck the risks will be less. Here are some other things you can do to lessen the risks:

- Set conditional terms – for example, you could make part of the price conditional upon a certain level of profits being achieved.
- Handcuff key employees – if most of the assets that you are buying are on two legs, then get service contracts or consultancy arrangements in place before the deal is signed.
- Non-competitive clauses – make sure that neither the seller nor their key employees can set up in competition, taking all the goodwill that you have just bought.
- Tax clearances – obviously you want to make sure that any tax losses that you are buying, or any tax implications in the purchase price, are approved by the Inland Revenue before committing yourself.
- Warranties and indemnities – if, after you have bought, you find there is a compulsory purchase order on the vendor's premises and the patent on their stunning new product is invalid, you would quite rightly be rather miffed. Warranties and indemnities set out those circumstances in which the seller will make good the buyer's financial loss. So if there is anything crucial that looks worrying, you could try to include it under this heading. Not unnaturally, the seller will resist.

Manage the acquisition

However well negotiated the deal, most acquisitions that go wrong do so because of the human factor – particularly in the first few weeks after the deal is made public. Some important rules to follow are these:

- Have an outline plan for how to handle the 'merger' – and be prepared to be flexible. (Interestingly enough, only one buyer in five has a detailed operational plan of how to manage their acquisition – but 67% of those being bought believe that the buyer has such a plan, so it is psychologically important.)

- ☐ Let business go on as usual for a few weeks, as you learn more about the internal workings of the company. Then you can make informed judgements on who or what should go or remain in post. This rule is followed by 90% of successful acquisitions.
- ☐ Hold management and staff meetings on day one, to clear up as much misunderstanding as you can. Do as much of this yourself as you possibly can.
- ☐ Never announce take-overs on a Friday. Staff will have all weekend to spread rumours. Wednesdays are best – just enough time to clear up misunderstandings, followed by a useful weekend breathing space.
- ☐ Make cuts/redundancies a once-only affair. It is always best to cut deep, and then get on with running a business. Continuous sackings sap morale, and all the best people will leave before it is their turn.
- ☐ Set limits of authority, reporting relationships, and put all banking relationships in the hands of your own accounts department, as quickly as possible.

The advantages of buying an existing business

- ☐ A going concern with a good history increases the likelihood of successful operation for the new owner.
- ☐ It has proved location for successful operation.
- ☐ The time, cost and energy required to do a thorough planning job for a new firm are eliminated. Profits can be earned sooner.
- ☐ It already has a proven customer base.
- ☐ It has an established relationship with suppliers, the business community and perhaps even bankers.
- ☐ Its equipment is already available, and its resources and capabilities are known in advance.
- ☐ Financing is restricted to a single sight transaction.

These advantages appear at first sight to be very significant. However, each must be studied very carefully in the individual case.

The disadvantages of buying an existing business

Even if these advantages stand the test of careful study, they should be weighed against the following important disadvantages:

- ☐ The buyer inherits any ill will of the existing firm.
- ☐ Sources of supplies are already established and may not conform to the buyer's best judgement.
- ☐ Employees may be inherited who are not up to standard.

- The inherited customer base may not be the most desirable, and changing the firm's image may be difficult.
- Precedents set by the former owner are well established and may be difficult to change.
- The building itself and the layout inside the firm may not conform to modern standards and may well be expensive to modernize.
- The landlords may be unhelpful.
- The purchase price may not be justified and may therefore deplete future profits.
- The price charged for the current stock may include slow-moving or obsolete merchandise.

Buying an existing firm does not always have all these disadvantages, but every firm being considered for purchase must be considered thoroughly.

Management buy-outs

This is a variation on the theme of buying out an existing business. The central concept is that the existing managers of a company buy it out from its owners. Many of the advantages and disadvantages of these strategies are the same. Buy-outs have a couple of very distinctive pluses. First, the business, its customers, competitors, suppliers and financial performance are well known to the buyers, as they have usually worked in or close to the company for several years. Second, the management team has worked together, and know one another's strengths and weaknesses. As they will be required to commit their personal wealth to the venture up to and beyond the threshold of pain, they can be counted on for their commitment.

One further advantage is that for 'social' reasons the business may be offered to the directors at a lower price than it would fetch on the open market.

The buy-out is usually effected by setting up a new company which buys either all, or more usually a part, of their old company. The money to do so is raised from banks, venture capital funds and from the managers themselves.

The reason for the buy-out often stems from the desire of the parent company to pull out of a certain activity, or to demerge from a previous amalgamation.

One of the most visible UK buy-outs was carried out by Sir Peter Thompson at the National Freight Corporation in 1982. One of the world's largest buy-out bids was made in October 1985 by the chairman of Macy and Co., the New York department store group, when he and his board offered £2.5 billion for the company.

In 1980 there were 100 management buy-outs in the United Kingdom, worth a total of £40 million. By the late 1990s the value of buy-outs had reached an annual £3.5 billion.

Various estimates put the number of UK buy-outs to date at rather more than 6,000. 3Is alone, who claim to have pioneered the technique, have completed over 1,000 (Figure 5.1). In Europe generally buy-outs have been much smaller in volume with the total for the whole continent being lower than the UK. France is something of an exception having the second highest buy-out activity level in Europe.

There are signs that as well as being numerous, buy-outs are a qualified success. Using a sample of 103 buy-outs (see Table 5.2), researchers at Nottingham University found that employment fell by 17% initially but later recovered to 95% of its original level over a period of two years. Over half the companies reported greater than expected profits and an improvement in sales. Over the period 1990 to the end of 1993, 381 buy-outs went into receivership and 443 were either floated on the stock market or sold on to a

Table 5.2 Sales and profit performance of buy-outs

	Number	Outcome
Sales	40	Substantial sales rise
	33	Slight sales rise
	16	No change
	12	Slight sales fall
	2	Major sales fall
Total sample	103	
Profits	58	Greater than expected
	11	As expected
	34	Less than expected
Total sample	103	

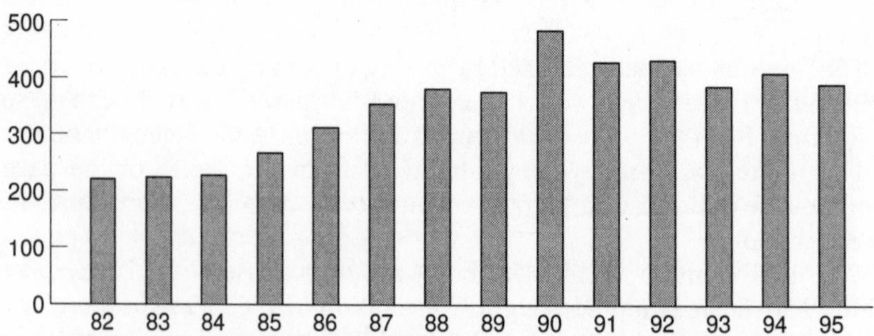

Figure 5.1 UK buy-outs 1982–95 (source: CMBOR/BZW Private Equity, Deloitte and Touche Corporate Finance, 1996).

non-management third party. Since 1989, when the buy-out failure rate was 13.1%, the failure rate has declined sharply to 3% or less.[4]

Buy-outs can also prove a useful exit route for small-business founders.

Example 5.3

Philip Green, aged 37, an Ayrshire (Scotland) farmer's son, has already made himself a sizeable fortune from building up and selling a company called Country Holidays before launching into the training business.

Country Holidays is basically an agency which lets country cottages to holiday makers. Philip Green launched it twelve years ago in Skipton and sold it in 1989 to the management for £14 million, retaining a 10% holding.

'Businesses have phases,' he says. 'Country Holidays reached the stage where it needed steady system management rather than the flat-out style of an entrepreneur.'

So Mr Green is now back in a two-roomed office in Skipton, putting his entrepreneurial talents to work in building his business. His selling tack is that most businesses need to improve their customer service and he can teach them how to do it.

Running the family business

If you are working in the family firm, and it is your aspiration to build up an enduring family business, then beware the old adage 'clogs to clogs in three generations'. In fact the average life cycle of a family business is twenty-four years, which coincides with the average tenure of the founder. Only 30% of family businesses reach the second generation and less than two-thirds of these survive through the second generation, while only 13% survive through the third generation!

Although these statistics illustrate the fragility of the continuing family business, you should not despair: more than 98% of US corporations, including some of the largest multinationals (Heinz and Campbell's Soup, for example), are family owned. In fact, about 42% of the largest companies are controlled by one person or family.

Family businesses have both strengths and weaknesses. By being aware of them you can exploit the former and do your best to overcome the latter to give your business a better chance of survival.

The overwhelming strength of the family business is the different atmosphere and feel that a family concern has. There can be a sense of belonging and common purpose which, more often than not, can lead to improved performance.

Another advantage is that a family firm has greater flexibility, since the unity of management and shareholders provides the opportunity to make quick decisions and to implement rapid change if necessary.

Potential problems

On the down side there are several weaknesses. Although these are not unique to family businesses, family firms are particularly prone to them. These are the main ones:

- *An unwillingness to respond to change.* This has been identified as the single most common cause of failure for family firms. The son of the founder of a car showroom chain, for example, had worked in the business, learning all aspects of the job. He had also learnt, however, that to please his father he should continue to do things in the same way as his father. So, when the son took over as manager he maintained the status quo. However, the expectation of the firm's customers had changed, the company did not respond and the firm failed.

  Resistance to change is also exacerbated by diminishing vitality as founders grow old. Also, too much reliance is often put on family management to the exclusion of outsiders, which may starve a growing firm of new ideas. A family firm may become inward-looking, insensitive to the message of the marketplace, unreceptive to outside ideas and unwilling to recruit competent outside managers.
- *Family goals and commercial goals may come into conflict.* For example, the shares of a family business are owned by the managing director and his two elderly aunts who rely on dividends from the firm to maintain them in a comfortable lifestyle. The managing director knows that investment in new machinery is essential for long-term prosperity but knows also that this would result in low dividends for the next five years. How can he choose a strategy that does not jeopardize either the firm's future or his aunts' comforts?

  Unlike other businesses, family firms have additional objectives to their financial performance targets. For example: building family reputation and status in the community; providing employment for the family; protecting the store of the family wealth; ensuring independence; a dynastic wish to pass on a position, in addition to wealth, to the next generation.

  However, superimposing these family values on the business can lead to difficulties. For example, nepotism may lead to the employment of family members at a level beyond their competence, or a salary above their worth, with resulting problems.
- *There may be a conflict between growth and ownership.* Entrepreneurs (founders) like to be in control and not answerable to anyone – usually they view the firm as an extension of themselves, and later-generation family managers, accustomed to operating in an environment where owner authority is unchallenged, also have a strong desire to be their own boss.

  The desire for total control may mean that the firm turns down the opportunity to grow because the family is reluctant to dilute its ownership. Family managers prefer majority ownership of a small company to minority holdings in a big company where they are answerable to other shareholders. Basically, a dilemma that all family managers face is one of either growing the company, keeping purely commercial goals in mind at whatever risk to family control, or to subordinate the firm's welfare to family constraints. Performance of family concerns is frequently handicapped by overreliance on family members and poor use of outsiders' skills. This affects all areas of the business, from recruitment through to management. It is common for members of a family to come to the firm demanding jobs and opportunities regardless of their competence, although employing people in this manner threatens the effectiveness and hence the very survival of the business. At management level, family pride will sometimes not allow a situation where its members are subordinate to an outsider – even if the outsider is a better person for the job.

Appraisal and training too are affected by family constraints. It is usually against family principles to engage in applying an objectively derived set of criteria to evaluate its members' worth. And on training, should family members be trained according to what is best for them as individuals, or according to what is best for the business? Regrettably, the two do not often coincide.

- *Many businesses fail to survive the process of succession from one chief executive to another.* Few people find it easy to come to terms with their own mortality and it may be hard for an entrepreneur to recognize the time when they are no longer the best person to run their firm. Very often businesses fail to plan for succession early enough; sometimes it is precipitated by death or ill-health – times when the family find it hard to give the matter the thought that it needs.

Some solutions

However, each of these areas of weakness can be tackled. Here are some tips for family businesses that want to retain their competitive edge and survive from one generation to the next.

- *Be outward looking and willing to change.* Where possible, family managers should be encouraged to build up experience outside the family firm and will often benefit from professional training. A manager who had successfully expanded his business school while his elder brother had remained in the firm explained his ability to offer the leadership needed thus: 'My brother had been working in the firm for years under my father. He couldn't conceive of any other way of doing things and eventually recognized he couldn't offer the same leadership and outside perspective.'

- *Establish an agreed set of family goals for the firm.* There should also be a clear statement of family policy on the employment of family members, succession and ownership. Also, the financial impact of the family's goals should be assessed. Managers in family businesses, like those in any other business, should be aware of their objectives and any conflicts between them.
- *Set up clear ownership objectives.* Examine the emotional factors behind ownership goals. The consequences of the dispersal of ownership should be fairly addressed and growth aspirations should be consistent with ownership objectives. Advice should be taken on the tax issues of passing ownership between generations. The family should adopt a commercial, dispassionate perspective in its relationships with staff and outsiders. Lastly, there should be a mechanism in place to reconcile the potential differences in outlook between family shareholders who work in the business and those who do not.
- *Reward and promote family employees strictly in line with their contribution to the firm.* Regular evaluations of the performance of all staff, including family members, should be instituted. Effective delegation is essential and businesses should work actively to attract and motivate high-quality outside managers, maybe using independent non-executive directors. The use of outside advisers is also sensible and is especially expedient today when the pace of change is so rapid. Many problems and issues are faced only once during the lifetime of a business. Going public, for example, is an event likely to occur only once. A specialist outsider can draw from a wider knowledge and make a positive contribution. None the less, many small businesses consistently fail to call them in.
- *Plan for succession early.* When doing so, firms should recognize the importance and psychological complexity of the succession process and use outside advisers to help them evaluate all the options. Clear requirements should be set for the selection and preparation of the successor.

Family businesses that address the five main areas discussed above will remain outward looking, responsive to change and able to generate lasting superior performance. Properly controlled family culture and the enhanced commitment by family members to the business will allow greater responsiveness, improved effectiveness and survival in a competitive and ever changing marketplace.

References

1. Rothwell, R., Freeman, C., Horsley, A., Jervis, V. T. P., Robertson, A. B. and Townsend, J., 'Project Sappho updated: project phase II', *Research Policy* **3**, 3 (1974), pp. 258–91.

2. Von Hippel, E. A., 'The dominant role of users in the scientific instrumentation innovation process', *Research Policy*, **5** (1976), pp. 212–39.
3. Madique, M. A. and Zirger, B. J., 'The new product learning cycle', *Research Policy*, **14**, 6 (1985), pp. 299–313.
4. 'Restructuring and failure in management buy-outs and buy-ins', *Strategy Review* (London: London Business School, 1994).

6

Franchising

Franchising is something of a half-way house, lying somewhere between entrepreneurship and employment. It holds many of the attractions of running a small business while at the same time eliminating some of the more unappealing risks. For example, the failure rate for both franchisors and franchisees (see Table 6.1) is low relative to the total franchise population and much lower than for the small business sector as a whole[1] which can range upwards of 30% (see Chapter 2).

Forms of franchising

Let us look at the various types of relationship between licensee and licensor which are described under the general heading 'franchises'.

A distributorship

This could be for a particular product, such as a make of car. It is also sometimes referred to as an agency, but there is a fundamental difference between these two concepts. An agent acts on behalf of a principal. Even though they are not employed by the principal, and even though they may have an agency for the products and services of more than one principal, what the agent does, says or represents to third parties is binding on the principal in question, as if they were employer and employee. A distributorship, however, is an arrangement where both parties are legally independent, as vendor and purchaser, except that the purchaser, in exchange for certain exclusive territorial rights, backed up by the vendor's advertising, promotion and,

Table 6.1 Unit changes reported by franchisors, by reason for change

	Changed franchisee	Bought back	Closed down	Sold/left franchising	Total
All reasons:	890	250	300	410	1850
Failure	80	30	140	85	335
Dispute	0	0	15	5	20
Other	810	220	145	320	1495

Source: British Franchise Association 1996 Survey.

possibly, training of their staff, will be expected to hold adequate stock and maintain their premises in a way that reflects well on the vendor's product or service.

A licence to manufacture

This applies to a certain product within a certain territory and over a given period of time. The licensee may have access to any secret process that this involves and can use the product's brand name in exchange for a royalty on sales.

This arrangement resembles a dictatorship. Licensor and licensee are independent of each other, except that the licensor will no doubt insist that the licensee complies with certain specifications as regards content and quality in order to preserve the good name of their product. The arrangement is often found in industry and two well-known examples have been the Rank Organisation's licence to produce the photocopying devices pioneered by the Xerox Corporation and the licences granted by Pilkington's for their revolutionary plate glass manufacturing process.

The use of a celebrity name

The name of a well-known person can be used to enhance the sales appeal of a product and guarantee, at least by implication, its quality.

The most common example is the endorsement, by a sports personality, of equipment associated with their activity and bearing their name, in return for a royalty payment by the manufacturer.

The realization that a 'personality' can sell things bearing their name came about principally through the exposure of sports in the media. In the 1930s there were some attempts to capitalize on movie stars' names in a similar way – an early poster associating Ronald Reagan with a brand of cigarettes has been much reprinted since he became prominent in another sphere – but sports men and women have been more ready, and perhaps better organized, to cash in on the advertising spin-off from the media coverage they get. A name can be franchised, at least for a while, to validate a product, particularly if there appears to be a direct connection between them: Arnold Palmer golf clubs, for instance.

The use of a trade mark

Here a widely recognized product is exploited commercially for a fee – subject to certain licensing conditions – rather than the name of an individual. An instance with which many readers will be familiar was Rubik's cube, always shown with the TM symbol beside it.

Business format franchising

Borrowed from the French, the term 'franchising' originally meant being free from slavery. Today, business format franchising is the name given to a relationship in which the owner of a product, a process or a service allows a local operator to set up a business under that name, for a specified period of time. The local operator (the franchisee) pays the parent organization (the franchisor) an initial fee and, usually, continuing royalties for the privilege.

The franchisor lays down a blueprint on how the business should be operated: the content and nature of the goods and services being offered, the price and quality of these goods, and even the location, size and layout of any premises to be used. The franchisor also provides the franchisee with training and other back-up support, such as accounting systems, advertising programmes and personnel recruitment and selection advice.

The growth of franchising

Sales from franchising now account for 25% of US Gross National Product, with sales exceeding $1 trillion, and operate out of some 350,000 business format franchise outlets.

In the United Kingdom the number of franchised outlets grew from 2,000 outlets to nearly 26,000 between 1980 and 1997. Sales now exceed £6 billion and more than 200,000 people are employed in the industry. Strong franchise sectors also exist in Japan, Canada, Australia, France and throughout most of Europe.

Although all the above forms of franchising continue to flourish, it could be said that business format franchising has emerged as the dominant and certainly the most rapidly expanding mode. This is because it meets the commercial needs of the present time. Looking back into the history of franchising for a moment, it is interesting to note that distributorship franchises were first applied to Singer sewing machines after the American Civil War when the United States emerged as a vast market, but when communications were too poor across great distances to make centralized distribution effective.

Contrary to popular opinion, the business format style of franchising did not begin with the boom of fast-food franchises such as McDonald's in the 1950s. In fact, franchising can date its beginnings back to the early 1800s. However, it was in 1898 that modern franchising really got under way when General Motors began franchising dealerships. Still alive and well today, their franchise system boasts 12,000 dealers scattered throughout the United States, and as many again throughout the world.

Franchise systems were also created by Rexall in 1902 and Howard Johnson in 1926 – as were many oil, grocery, motel and fast-food franchises during those years. So great has been its growth that most industries have already been touched by franchising. According to the American National Federation of Independent Business, about 10% of the nation's 18 million businesses now run under some kind of franchise agreement.

In essence, franchising thrives because it merges the incentive of owning a business with the management skills of big business. And personal ownership is one of the best incentives yet created to spur hard work.

Franchising may benefit not only the franchisee but also the franchisor. For example, it may enable the franchisor to grow rapidly by using other people's (i.e. the franchisee's) money. That is largely how giant franchisors like McDonald's and Baskin-Robbins have mushroomed into billion-dollar businesses in so short a time.

The idea that franchisees are independent business people is something of a myth. Franchisees generally are not free to run their business as they see fit. They are often hamstrung by the franchisor's policies, standards and procedures. Nor do franchisors encourage their franchisees to improve the way they do business. To quote the Bank of America: 'The best franchisee, as far as many franchisors are concerned, is someone who is smart enough to understand and operate the system, but not smart enough to try to improve on it.'

One franchisor describes the ideal franchisee as the sergeant type – midway between the general who gives the orders, and the private who merely follows them. People who want their own business to escape taking orders from others frequently see franchising as the answer. They are subsequently frustrated by lack of autonomy.

The business sectors covered by franchising

In the 1990s, in the United Kingdom the largest fields of activity in terms of systems units are business services (23%), home improvements (13%), property maintenance (9%), health and beauty (8%) and leisure (7%).

Food, divided up between fast food and 'other' food, accounts for a total of 15%, but when you look at turnover percentages, a significantly different picture emerges. The percentage of turnover accounted for by fast foods is in line with the percentage of units (7%), but 'other' foods, which has 8% of the total number of systems, accounts for no less than 22% of industry turnover, only just behind business services with 24% of turnover. By contrast, home improvement, the second biggest in the number of units, only accounts for 5% of turnover. This suggests that one of the factors to look out for in choosing a franchise is not so much the number of units in operation, but the turnover (and, of course, the profitability) per unit.

The factors that fuelled the growth of franchising in the 1980s were equally divided between changes in the economic and political climate. The recessions of the 1980s and early 1990s generated more people with large redundancy payments, who elected for self-employment rather than a fruitless search for a job. This view is supported by the rapid acceleration of older people starting up a business. In 1988 around 13% of business starters were aged 45 and over. By 1995 this proportion had grown to 21%.[2] Franchising seemed to offer a way of combining the independence of self-employment with the security of a proven business formula. Independence and security from unemployment are consistently rated as the two prime motivators for starting up a business.[3] The late 1990s see many of these factors still at play in many countries. Downsizing, or its many euphemisms, and an unwillingness of many firms to recruit the over 45s look like being around for a while yet. Market factors have helped too. Changed lifestyles have made fast food more acceptable. The growing numbers of women entering work has fuelled a demand for dry cleaning services, home help agencies and convenience stores with long opening hours.

The simplest form and usually the cheapest to acquire is a job franchise service which is run from home, a cleaning service, for instance, or a vehicle maintenance franchise such as Hometune. Much the largest group of franchises, however, are those that entail acquiring premises and often a substantial investment in equipment in addition to the initial fee payable to the franchisor: fast-food restaurants and print shops are two of the most visible and widespread franchises of this type.

At the top end of the market are investment franchises like Holiday Inn, where the start-up costs can run well into six figures. Overall, the range of activities that can be franchised is very wide and some sixty-five have been identified in the United States, ranging from hotel ownership at the top end to a soft-drink bottling franchise with the unlikely name of Cock 'n Bull Ltd at the other. The latter is an indication that not all American enterprises can be readily transplanted into the international market. There are at the moment at least forty types of franchise in Britain, covering a wide variety of fields from fast food to dry cleaning.

In the United States large franchisors – those with 1,000 or more units each – dominate business format franchising, with 57 companies accounting for 53% of sales and 55% of establishments. These figures should be viewed against a backdrop of over 4,000 franchisors operating in 50 business sectors in this market, employing some 7 million people between them.

Only 70% of outlets in franchise chains in North America are franchisee operated. The remainder are company-owned stores using hired managers. These 'company stores' are acknowledged to be less profitable than franchised outlets.

In general, franchising is viewed as being a relatively 'safe' way into business with only a small fraction of a per cent of the country's 350,000+ franchises failing in any one year. There is also evidence that franchisees are generally satisfied with their lot. Some 90% sign up again when the term of their agreement expires.

The main growth in US business format franchising is in the service sector, encouraged in part by the low cost of entry compared with established car repair and fast-food franchises. This high-growth sector includes such areas as the following:

- Financial counselling services.
- Home repair.
- Insurance.
- Legal services centres.
- Accounting services centres.
- Medical services.
- Dental clinics.
- Business brokers.
- Weight reduction centres.
- Figure control centres.
- Smoking control centres.
- Exercise studios.
- Safe deposit box locations.

Many of these activities are either in their infancy or non-existent in the UK franchise market. Restrictive practices permitting, it seems inevitable that these types of franchise will make their presence more strongly felt in the United Kingdom in the coming decade.

Advantages and disadvantages of taking up a franchise

The advantages and disadvantages of taking up a franchise depend to some extent on the content of the agreement, but there is a core of balancing factors which are largely common because they relate to the nature of the kind of activity that franchising involves.

The franchisor

Advantages

From the franchisor's point of view, the advantages are that they do not have any direct investment in an outlet bearing their name. The inventory and equipment are owned by the franchisee. Because of the shortage of prime sites, there is a growing trend for franchisors to acquire leases on behalf of franchisees, or at any rate to stand as guarantors. Nevertheless, the effect on the liquidity of the franchisor, in contrast to expansion by opening branches, is enormous – although if they do their job properly there are heavy start-up costs in piloting the franchise and in setting up and maintaining training. Thereafter there are further costs in providing a continuing service to franchisees in such matters as research and development, promotion, administrative back-up and feedback and communication within the network. The expectation is that these costs will be offset by the fact that the franchisee, as the owner of the business, is more likely to be highly motivated than an employee and more responsive to local market needs and conditions; that the franchisor receives an income from the franchise; that they save on personnel and administrative costs; and that, without direct financial involvement, they may in this way derive some of the benefits of expansion, in as much as franchising provides economies of scale from centralized purchasing and, if they wished it and it is feasible, some degree of centralized administrative facilities.

Disadvantages

The disadvantages are that, although the failure of an individual franchise may reflect badly on the franchise operation as a whole, all the franchisor can control is the format itself and they can only influence the running of individual operations by pulling the reins on this or that clause in the agreement – the broad terms of which we shall discuss shortly. In extreme cases the franchisor may terminate the agreement or at any rate not renew it, but they cannot throw the franchisee out as if they were the employee. The franchisor is therefore dependent on the willingness of the franchisee to observe the rules and play the game, while at the same time any failure to do so is equally, and perhaps more, damaging to the franchisor (and to other franchisees) than to the franchisee concerned because of its adverse effects on the franchise as a whole.

Another disadvantage sometimes turns out to lie in the curious mixture of dependence and independence that franchising produces. The franchisee is encouraged to think of themselves as an independent business entity, and to a large extent this is indeed the situation. Nevertheless, they are operating the franchisor's business concept under a licence for which a fee is payable. There are cases where a franchisee identifies so closely with the particular business they are running that they ultimately resent the payment of the fee. The success is felt to be due to the franchisee's own effort, not to the franchise concept or to the franchisor. This is apt to be particularly so if the franchisor adopts a lower profile than they should, either in terms of direct help or in matters such as national advertising. Clearly, of course, the franchisee would be obliged to pay under the terms of the agreement, but a sour relationship is not good for either party, so it is up to the franchisor to maintain their part of the bargain both in letter and in spirit. Franchises are a matter of mutual interests and obligations.

The franchisee

From the point of view of the franchisee, also, there are advantages and disadvantages which might, perhaps, be most clearly expressed in the form of a list.

Advantages

- A business format or product which has already been market tested and, presumably, been found to work. As a consequence, major problems can be avoided in the start-up period.
- A recognized name of which the public is already aware and which has credibility with the suppliers.
- Publicity, both direct, in that the franchisor advertises their product or services, and indirect promotion through signage and other corporate image promotion in all the franchisor's outlets.
- Although taking up a franchise is not cheaper than starting on your own, it is considered that the percentage of expensive errors made by individuals starting on their own is substantially reduced by the adoption of a tested format.
- Direct and close assistance during the start-up period.
- A period of training on production and management aspects.
- A set of standard management, accounting, sales and stock control procedures incorporated in an operating manual.

- Better terms for centralized bulk purchase negotiated through the franchisor, although they may be looking for mark-ups in this area as a source of revenue from the franchise.
- The benefit of the franchisor's research and development in improving the product.
- Feedback throughout the network on operating procedures and the facility to compare notes with other franchisees, both formally and informally.
- Design of the premises to an established scheme saves on interior design fees and may eliminate these altogether where the franchisor has a set of specifications.
- The benefit of the franchisor's advice on equipment selection and initial inventory levels, although this may be partial where the franchisor is also the supplier.
- Help with site selection, negotiating with planning officers and developers.
- Possibly, though not universally, access to the franchisor's legal and financial advisers.
- The protected or privileged rights to the franchise within a given area.
- Improved prospects of obtaining loan facilities from the bank.
- The backing of a known trading name when negotiating for good sites with letting agents or building owners.

Disadvantages

- Business format franchising is, of necessity, something of a cloning exercise. There is virtually no scope for individual initiative in matters of product, service or design. However, the franchisor will demand uniformly high standards of maintenance, appearance and packaging in whatever the franchise entails. These are usually monitored by regular inspection.
- The royalty (sometimes called a management fee) paid to the franchisor. This is usually based on gross turnover or on profit. The problem here is that if the franchisor is not pulling their weight, or if the franchisee does not feel this to be the case, the royalty can be subject to bitter dispute. The franchisee may then feel justified in withholding all or part of it on the grounds of non-performance by the franchisor, but this is always a difficult matter to prove in the courts. Furthermore, the franchisor's resources to conduct a long drawn-out case will usually be greater than the franchisee's.
- A further problem is that a high turnover does not necessarily imply a highly profitable operation. If the franchisor's income is wholly or partially

based on turnover, they may try to push for this at the expense of profitability. The franchisee is not absolutely at liberty to sell the franchise even though they are in many respects operating the business independently. The sale has to be approved by the franchisor, who is also entitled to vet the vendor and charge the cost of any investigations made to the existing franchise. Furthermore, although the business would be valued as a going concern, in trading terms the goodwill remains the property of the franchisor. Again, the franchisee may feel that, at least to some extent, the goodwill has been built up by their own efforts. The resale of a franchise, in other words, is a process rich in those grey areas that can lead to expensive litigation.

- Territory agreements may be difficult to enforce in practice. For instance, the hypothetical firm of Calorie Countdown may have the exclusive rights in the suburb in which it is located, but there is nothing to prevent the citizens of that suburb from buying their slimmer's meals in some other neighbouring Calorie Countdown outlet.
- The franchisee, as well as paying a royalty to the franchisor, may be obliged to buy goods and services from them as well – possibly at disadvantageous rates.
- Although the franchisor places all sorts of controls and obligations on the franchisee to maintain the quality of their image, the scope for doing the reverse is more limited. If the franchisor's products or service gets bad publicity, this is bound to affect the franchisee adversely, and there is very little they could do about it. Equally, the franchisor may engage in promotional activities (and involve the franchisee in them as well) which, though perfectly harmless, may, from the point of view of a particular outlet, be an irrelevant waste of time.
- The failure of a franchisor may leave the franchisee with a business that is not viable in isolation.

From this list it will be clear that the franchise contract between franchisor and franchisee is a vital document. Its construction can make or break the relationship.[4]

A mutual dependence

From this list of advantages and disadvantages to both parties a more detailed picture emerges of the business format franchise as a relationship of mutual dependence which allows each party to realize their strength to their mutual and, at best, equal advantage.

The franchisor is able to expand without further investment and, although the return is obviously lower than from expansion by ownership, they do receive an income from the franchisee as well as getting both an outlet for their product and more muscle in negotiating the purchase of materials and equipment. The franchisee, on the other hand, is able to concentrate their entrepreneurial skills at the sharp end of sales and customer service, while the administrative headaches of setting up the business are mitigated by the uniform nature of the format. By the same token they are saved, through feedback to the franchisor of the accumulated experience of the franchises, from making the errors to which businesses are prone in their early and most vulnerable stages. This relationship is expressed as agreements – the purchase agreement and the franchise agreement. But before considering these, it is necessary to evaluate the franchise as a whole.

A study by Professor Russell M. Knight of the University of Western Ontario (see Table 6.2) illustrates the close agreement between franchisees and franchisors on the advantages of franchising, although, in general, franchisees were slightly less enthusiastic. But much of the advantage of franchising lies in getting franchisees with appropriate characteristics.

A study of the personal franchisee characteristics required for success (see Table 6.3), also carried out by Professor Russell M. Knight of the University of Western Ontario, concluded that franchisees and franchisors have a large measure of agreement on what makes for success.

They disagreed only in rating management ability and creativity – a point that may provide some clues as to what franchisors are really looking for in a franchise.

Table 6.2 The advantages of franchising

	Franchisees in agreement %	Franchisors in agreement %
You can make more money in a franchise than in an independent business	51	47
A franchise is less risky than going it alone	78	88
A franchise offers greater job satisfaction than salaried employment	95	82
A franchise offers more independence than salaried employment	92	83
A franchise offers a proven business formula	83	99
A franchise offers the benefit of a known trade name	96	99
You can develop a franchise more quickly than an independent business	92	86

Table 6.3 Personal franchisee characteristics required for success

	Franchisee %			Franchisor %		
	Very important	Important	Not important	Very important	Important	Not important
Previous management experience in same industry	0	20	80	2	14	84
Previous own-business experience	12	46	42	16	47	37
Management ability	84	15	1	66	31	3
Desire to succeed	90	10	0	93	7	0
Willingness to work hard	92	8	0	93	6	1
Creativity	26	56	18	12	44	44
Strong people skills	63	32	5	64	34	2
Financial backing	71	27	2	67	27	6
Support from family	52	28	20	46	32	22

Note: Study size – 148 franchisors and 105 franchisees replied to questionnaire with follow-up interviews with 25 members of each group.

Women in franchising

The trend toward more involvement by women among recent recruits has been maintained: 26% of all new franchisees in 1995 were women, compared with 22% three years earlier.[5]

References

1. Power, M., *Business Format Franchisees: Closing or Continuing* (London: Power Research Associates, 1993).
2. *Starting up in business*, Barclays Research on Small Business Characteristics, Barclays Bank plc, United Kingdom, 1995.
3. *Office World Quarterly Small Business Survey*, **2**, 1, Globus Office World plc in association with the Small Business Research Centre, September (1995).
4. Mendelson, M., *A Guide to Franchising* (Eastbourne: Cassell, 1993).
5. National Westminster Bank, British Franchise Association 1996 survey.

7

Market research

The Duke of Wellington called reconnaissance 'the art of knowing what is on the other side of the hill'. Market research is the business equivalent of that activity.

Market research is the name given to the process of collecting, recording, classifying and analyzing data on customers, competitors and any other factors influencing the buying claim. It is the breadth of the gulf between a new business and its customers that makes this information-gathering so vital.

Entrepreneurs are often deterred by the rigours of market research, or simply do not know how to carry it out cheaply. They rely instead on their own subjective judgement; they develop the iceberg syndrome, believing that the small number of customers they can see are a sure indication of the mass of other customers. It is a fundamental mistake to believe that people are simply waiting to be sold to and that competitors are blind or lazy. The first vital role of market research is 'market positioning'. Sometimes referred to as finding 'niches',[1] or 'interstices'.[2] This concentration on entering a niche market emerges as one of the key factors influencing the success of small-business strategies.[3] Many research studies, including those referred to above, argue that the different growth rates experienced in different markets, for example a booming computer sector and a depressed housing sector, have less impact on the performance of a small firm than the buoyancy of the highly specific market in which it operates. So new businesses need a clear and detailed picture of their market well before they launch.

The range of possible research topics is wide, and what is appropriate to one business could be irrelevant to another. However, there are certain questions that need to be answered by more or less all potential businesses.

Market research topics

Where is my market?

The starting-point in any market appreciation has to be a definition of the scope of the market you are aiming for. A small general shop may only service the needs of a few dozen streets. A specialist restaurant will have to call on a much larger catchment area.

You may eventually decide to sell to different markets. For example, a retail business can serve a local area through the shop and a national area by mail order. A small manufacturing business could branch out into exporting.

People all too often flounder in initial market research by describing their markets too broadly: for example, saying that they are in the motor industry when they really mean second-hand car sales in Perth.

While it is helpful to know about the trends in the wider market, this must not obscure the need to focus on the precise area that you have to serve.

How big is that market? You need some idea of the market size in order to work out how much you can realistically expect to sell. If you were in the home improvements market, your calculations might run as follows: on average, people in the United Kingdom spend £11 per year on home improvements products; so if the catchment population for a retail outlet is 25,000 people, the total market potential for that area is £11 × 25,000 = £275,000. Using the same data for previous years, you can work out how fast the market is expanding or contracting.

Who are my competitors?

Most businesses have competitors. To some extent this is reassuring because you know in advance that customers need what you have to offer. But you have to identify who they are and how they can affect your business. You have to know everything about them and their strengths and weaknesses; their product range, prices, discount structure, delivery arrangements, specifications, minimum order quantities and terms of trade. The competitive nature of the marketplace into which a firm sells is a key influence on the strategies that it should adopt. A hostile, highly competitive marketplace calls for flexibility and risk-taking. A benign, less competitive environment, calls for more emphasis on systems and procedures.[4] But whichever the environment, research by Westhead and Birly[5] has shown clearly that low-growth firms have the poorest understanding of their competitors.

How can I differentiate my business from the competition?

There has to be something unique about either you or your product that makes you stand out from your competitors. It could be something as obvious as being open later or longer. Or it may be a policy, such as the John Lewis Partnership's 'never knowingly undersold' message. Whatever your unique selling proposition is, communicate it effectively.

What should I charge?

The greatest danger in setting a price for the first time is to pitch it too low. Raising a price is always more difficult than lowering one. There are great temptations to undercut the competition at the outset.

Every product or service has its own demand curve, relating sales volume to selling price, showing that the lower the price, the greater the quantity sold. This can help you think out how a change in price will affect your sales volume.

The sensitivity of demand to price is called 'price elasticity'. If demand increases more than proportionally when a product price is reduced, then the demand is elastic. If it does not, it is not elastic. Sales of Rolls-Royce cars are not likely to be improved significantly by lowering prices. In fact, the snob appeal may be diminished, so this is an inelastic demand curve. You have quickly to get a feel for how your sales volume is affected by price changes.

What is my message and where is the medium?

Lord Leverhulme is reported to have said that half the money he spent on advertising was wasted, but no one could tell him which half. A key element in your marketing strategy has to be what to tell whom and how to tell them.

If you start off by deciding how many people you want to influence, and what you want them to do as a result of seeing your advertisement, then you are off to a good start. In some media, response ratios are well established. For example, planning for more than a 2% response from a direct mail shot would be unrealistic.

Developing a product market strategy

People starting a new business almost always define their product in physical terms. Customers, on the other hand, want their needs satisfied. Compare a Bic and a Parker pen. In basic physical terms they are very similar. They both write well; their caps protect your pocket from ink stains; both have clips that hold them in place; and they are comfortable to grip. But one costs around 10p and the other from about £3.00. Customers pay the extra £2.90 for largely intangible benefits such as status, or the pleasure that the pen will bring as a gift. Bic and Parker are both successful products, but the needs they satisfy are poles apart. Customers' needs must be defined before the business can begin to assemble a product to satisfy them.

Name names

Without customers, no business can get off the ground, let alone survive. Some people believe that customers arrive after the firm 'opens its doors'. This is clearly nonsense. A business needs customers before it can even think of launching. The customers themselves are a vital part of a successful business strategy, and are not simply the passive recipients of new products or services. Even those ventures that start off with a handful of clients, perhaps poached from a previous employer, need the certainty of a wider customer base if they are to survive and prosper. Overdependence on a few important customers is an all too common problem for the new business. The Bolton Committee Report,[6] published in 1971, confirmed that small firms in general were highly dependent on a single customer or a small number of customers. Twenty years later, the Cambridge Small Business Research Centre[7] confirmed that one in three small firms relied on one customer for more than a quarter of their sales. That this is a highly dangerous situation was confirmed in the Westhead and Birley study, referred to above. These researchers demonstrated that the fastest growing small firms were those with the widest customer base.

Naming names of customers, both actual and potential, is a start, but then these customers must be looked at in terms of the group or category into which they fall. For example, train users divide into commuters and off-peak travellers: those who have to get to a certain destination by a certain time, and those who do not. The relative intensity of need allows a premium price to be charged to the former and a price incentive is offered to the latter to induce them away from using their cars.

Satisfy needs

When asked what his business did, the founder of a successful cosmetics firm replied, 'In the factories we make perfume and in the shops we sell dreams.' This same philosophy is true of every product or service.

Maslow,[8] the eminent American psychologist, suggested that 'all customers are goal-seekers who gratify their needs by purchase and consumption'.

He classified consumer needs in a five-stage pyramid known as the 'hierarchy of needs'. The first and the greatest need was physiological (hunger and thirst), followed by safety, social, self-esteem and, at the top of the pyramid, self-realization. Every product or service is bought to satisfy one or more of these needs. So, for example, as people's hunger and thirst needs are satisfied, they move up the hierarchy, to satisfy other needs.

Defining the product market strategy

Everyone needs a purpose in their lives to make it worthwhile and rewarding. A business also needs a purpose to keep it headed in the right direction, amid the welter of distractions that threaten to divert even the most dedicated entrepreneur from their other chosen goal. That purpose should be defined as simply as possible in terms of what the business does and for whom it does it.

For example, Blooming Marvellous, a competitor to Mothercare, founded in 1980 by two young mothers-to-be, and now a £2 million business, defines its activities as follows: 'We design, make and market clothes for the fashion-conscious mother-to-be.' This statement is proof that the business has defined its product/market strategy and knows exactly where it is going. With the same skills they could market clothes for children, or for women who were not pregnant, but pursuing these markets would dilute their scarce resources, leaving them vulnerable and open to attack on too many fronts.

Some further product issues

Is one product enough?

One-product businesses are the natural output of the inventor, but they are extremely vulnerable to competition, changes in fashion and to technological obsolescence. Having only one product can also limit the growth potential of the enterprise. Several of the following examples focus on the aspirations of businesses in this situation: a question mark must inevitably hang over them until they can broaden out their product base.

- *Single-sale products.* Medsoft, a start-up business, focused on selling micro-computers and a tailor-made software package to hospital doctors. Unfortunately the management had no idea of the cost and effort required to sell each unit. Worse still, there were no repeat sales. It was not that customers did not like the product: they did, but each user needed only one product. This meant that all the money and time spent on building up a 'loyal' customer was largely wasted. In another type of venture, for example selling company cars, you could reasonably expect a satisfied customer to come back every two or three years. In the restaurant business the repeat cycle might be every two to three months.

- *Non-essential products.* Entrepreneurs tend to be attracted to fad, fashion and luxury items because of the short response time associated with their promotion and sale. Companies producing for these markets frequently run into financial difficulties arising out of sudden market shifts. Market security is more readily gained by having products that are viewed as 'essential'.
- *Too simple a product.* Simplicity, usually a desirable feature, can be a drawback. If a business idea is so basic that little management or marketing expertise is required for success, this is likely to make the cost of entry low and the value added minimal. This makes it easy for every Tom, Dick or Harry to duplicate the product idea, and impossible for the original company to defend its market, except by lowering its price.

  The video rental business was a classic example of the 'too simple product' phenomenon. Too many people jumped on the bandwagon as virtually anyone with a couple of thousand pounds could set themselves up. Rental prices fell from pounds to pence in a year or so, and hundreds of businesses folded.

DIY market research

The purpose of practical DIY market research – for 'entrepreneurs' investigating or seeking to start a new business – is therefore twofold:

1. To build *credibility* for the business idea, the entrepreneur must prove first to their own satisfaction, and later to that of outside financiers, a thorough understanding of the marketplace for the new product or service. This will be vital if resources are to be attracted to build the new venture.
2. To develop a *realistic* market entry strategy for the new business, based on a clear understanding of genuine customer needs and ensuring that product quality, price, promotional methods and distribution chain are mutually supportive and clearly focused on target customers.

Research, above all else, is not just essential in starting a business but, once launched, it must become an integral part in the ongoing life of the company. Customers and competitors change; products have life cycles. Once started, however, ongoing market research becomes easier, as you will have existing customers (and staff) to question. It is important that you monitor regularly their views on your business.

First steps

There are two main types of research in starting a business:

- □ Desk research, or the study of published information.
- □ Field research, involving fieldwork in collecting specific information for the market.

Both activities are vital for the starter business.

Desk research

There is increasingly a great deal of secondary data, available in published form and accessible via business sections of public libraries throughout the most developed countries to enable new starters both to quantify the size of market sectors they are entering and to determine trends in those markets. In addition to populations of cities and towns (helping to start quantification of markets), libraries frequently purchase reports involving studies of growth in different business sectors. Government statistics showing trends in the economy and in individual sectors are also held.

It is important that business founders can demonstrate that their sector is growing (is the wind behind you, like Anita Roddick with the 'green' movement behind her 'natural' beauty products?), or if the sector is declining, can it be demonstrated why a product/service will be different and will not be affected by the trend (e.g. although in the United Kingdom car manufacturing has declined, the makers of 'kit cars' have focused on a growing profitable niche of 'enthusiasts')?

Field research

For example, in contemplating opening a classical music shop in Exeter, focused on the young, desk research revealed that out of a total population of 250,000 there is 25% of under 30-year-olds, but it did not state what percentage are interested in classical music or how much they might spend on classical records. Field research (questionnaire in street) provided the answer of 1% and £2 a week spent, suggesting a potential market of only £65,000 a year (250,000 × 25% × 1% × £2 × 52!). The entrepreneurs sensibly decided to investigate Birmingham and London instead!

But at least the cost had been only two damp afternoons spent in Exeter, rather than the horror of having to dispose of the lease of an unsuccessful shop.

Fieldwork is now becoming quite big business. In the United Kingdom alone expert market research companies turned over more than £400 million a year. Most fieldwork carried out consists of interviews, with the interviewer putting the questions to a respondent. We are all becoming accustomed to it, whether being interviewed while travelling, or resisting the attempts of enthusiastic salespeople posing as market researchers on doorsteps ('sugging', as this is known, has been illegal since 1986). The more popular forms of interviews ranked in order are:

- Personal (face-to-face) interviews account for about half of all interviews (especially for consumer markets).
- Telephone surveys account for over a third of this market.
- Postal surveys and focus and discussion groups are about equally matched, and make up the balance of the 'interview' types.

Personal interviews and postal surveys are clearly less expensive than getting together panels of interested parties or using expensive telephone time. Telephone interviewing requires a very positive attitude, courtesy, an ability not to talk too quickly and listening while sticking to a rigid questionnaire. Low response rates on postal surveys (less than 10% is normal) can be improved by accompanying letters, explaining purpose and why respondents should reply, by offering rewards for completed questionnaires (small gift), by sending reminder letters, by making the first questions of particular interest to respondents and, of course, by providing pre-paid reply envelopes.

All methods of approach require considered questions. In drawing up the questionnaire , attention must be paid first to the following:

- Defining your research objectives; what exactly is it that you need vitally to know (e.g. how often do people buy, how much?)?
- Who are the customers to sample for this information (e.g. for DIY products, an Ideal Home Exhibition crowd might be best)?
- How are you going to undertake the research (e.g. face-to-face in street)?

When you are sure of the above, and only then, you are ready to design the questionnaire. There are six simple rules to guide this process:

1. Keep the number of questions to a minimum.
2. Keep the questions simple! Answers should be either Yes/No/Don't Know, or offer at least four alternatives.
3. Avoid ambiguity – make sure that the respondent really understands the question (avoid 'generally', 'usually', 'regularly').

4. Seek factual answers; avoid opinions.
5. Make sure at the beginning that you have a cut-out question, to eliminate unsuitable respondents (e.g. those who never use the product/service).
6. At the end, make sure that you have an identifying question to show a cross-section of respondents.

The size of the survey undertaken is also important. You frequently hear of political opinion polls taken on samples of 1,500–2,000 voters. This is because the accuracy of your survey increases with the size of sample, as Table 7.1 shows.

So if, on a sample size of 600, your survey showed that 40% of women in the town drove cars, the true proportion probably lies between 36% and 44%. For small businesses, a minimum sample of 250 is recommended.

Remember above all, however, that questioning is by no means the only or most important form of fieldwork. Sir Terence Conran, when questioned on a radio programme, inferred that he undertook no market research fieldwork at all (i.e. formal interviews). Later in the programme he confessed, none the less, to spending nearly 'half of his time visiting competitors, inspecting new and rival products, etc.'. Visiting exhibitions, buying and examining competitors' products (as the Japanese have so painfully done, in disassembling competitive cars piece by piece, deciding in the process where cost-effective improvements could be made) are clearly important fieldwork processes.

Just as importantly, test marketing by selling at stalls on a Saturday, or taking part in an exhibition, gives an opportunity to question interested customers and can be the most valuable fieldwork of all. All methods are equally valid, and the results of each should be carefully recorded for subsequent use in presentations and business plans.

Once the primary market research (desk and field research) and market testing (stalls and exhibitions) are complete, pilot testing of the business should take place in one location or customer segment before going for a full business launch.

Table 7.1 Estimation of survey accuracy

With random sample of . . .	95% of surveys are right within . . . points
250	6.2
500	4.4
750	3.6
1,000	3.1
2,000	2.2
6,000	1.2

References

1. Bradburd, R. M. and Ross, D. R., 'Can small firms find and defend strategic niches? A test of the Porter Hypothesis', *Review of Economics and Statistics*, **LXXI**, 2 (May 1989), pp. 258–62.
2. Penrose, E. T., *The Theory of the Growth of the Firm* (London: Basil Blackwell, 1959).
3. Wingham, D. L. and Kelmar, J. H., *Factors of Small Business Success Strategies*, School of Management Working Paper 92.01, Curtin University of Technology, Perth, Western Australia, 1992.
4. Colvin, J. G. and Slevin, D. P., 'Strategic management of small firms in hostile and benign environments', *Strategic Management Journal*, **10**, 1989, pp. 75–87.
5. Westhead, P. and Birley, S., *Employment Growth in New Independent Owner-managed Firms in Great Britain*, University of Warwick, 1993.
6. Bolton, J. E., *Report of the Committee of Enquiry on Small Firms*, Cmnd 4811 (London: HMSO, 1971).
7. Cambridge Small Business Research Centre, *The State of British Enterprise* (Department of Applied Economics, University of Cambridge, 1992).
8. Maslow, A., *Motivation and Personality* (New York: Harper & Row, 1954).

8

Financial management

All businesses need sound financial management – and small firms are no exception to that rule. Proper management accounts with pro forma cash flows, profit and loss accounts and balance sheets are essential if a firm is to survive and prosper, as is variance analysis comparing what was planned with what actually occurred. Accounting procedures are, to say the least, patchy in small firms. A study in 1994[1] of 200 small firms in the United Kingdom, revealed that only 34% used any form of budgeting and 16% of firms with debtors kept no debtor records. The study also showed that firms that were performing satisfactorily or better were those firms most likely to keep the best accounting records.

However, there are aspects of financial management that cause particular problems for small firms.

Winning the cash-flow war

Most business founders think that their problems are over once customers start to roll in. Unfortunately, they may have only just begun. One of the characteristics that most new or small businesses have in common is a tendency to change their size and shape quickly. In the early weeks and months customers are few, and each new customer (or a particularly big order) can mean a large percentage increase in sales.

A large increase in sales in turn means an increase in raw materials and perhaps more wages and other expenses. Generally, these expenses have to be met before your customer pays up. But until the money comes in, the business has to find cash to meet its bills. If it cannot find the cash to meet these day-to-day bills, the business very often goes bankrupt.

Bankers have a name for it. They call it overtrading. It means taking on more business than you have the cash to finance. Consider this example.

Example 8. 1

High Note is a new music shop selling sheet music, instruments, classical records and cassettes. Customers include schools and colleges who expect trade credit, and members of the public who pay cash. The owner put in £10,000 and borrowed a further £10,000 from his bank. When he started up these seemed enough funds to meet the £12,500 bill for shop fixtures and fittings, and the opening stock of £5,500.

As people heard about him and his reputation grew, he expected sales to build up to a satisfactory level. In any case, he felt that he could rely on his cash customers to meet his day-to-day expenses and any increases in stock. But he had reckoned without calculating the effect on cash flow of paying on the nail for supplies, and having to give trade credit, while his sales were growing rapidly.

He opened in April. By the middle of June he had run out of cash, and by August he needed an overdraft equivalent to 30% of the entire capital of the business. What was particularly galling was that the growth in sales exceeded his wildest dreams.

The cash picture over the first few months is set out in Table 8.1. The top of this cash picture shows the sales as they were achieved and the percentage rate of sales growth. Below that is the cash that comes in from the customers. (In the first month the start-up capital is also coming in.)

From May, when credit sales began, the gap between sales achieved and cash coming in grew rapidly. This was because purchases of stock had to stay in line with the growth in sales

Table 8.1 The cash picture

	April	May	June	July	Aug.	Sept.
	ACTUAL RESULTS			FORECASTS		
	£	£	£	£	£	£
Sales achieved	4,000	6,000	7,000	9,000	15,000	19,000
Sales growth	70% PER MONTH					27%
Sales receipts	4,000	5,000	6,000	7,000	12,000	15,000
Owner's capital	10,000					
Loan capital	10,000					
Total cash in	24,000	5,000	5,000	7,000	12,000	15,000
Cash payment out						
Purchases	5,500	2,950	4,220	7,416	9,332	9,690
Rent/rates, etc.	2,300	2,300	2,300	2,300	2,300	2,300
Wages	1,000	1,000	1,000	1,000	1,000	1,000
Advertising	250	250	250	250	250	250
Fixtures and fittings	12,500					
Total cash out	21,550	6,500	7,770	10,966	12,882	13,240
Cash balances						
Monthly cash balance	2,450	(1,500)	(2,770)	(3,966)	(882)	1,760
Balance brought forward	–	2,450	950	(1,820)	(5,786)	(6,668)
Balance to carry forward or net cash flow	2,450	950	(1,820)	(5,786)	(6,668)	(4,908)

achieved, and not with the cash coming in. So, for example, in July High Note actually paid out more for stock than it received in cash. And the overheads had still to be paid.

What High Note's worried owner did not know in August was that his negative cash flow had peaked. As average monthly sales growth slowed down from a meteoric 70% between April and August to a more modest 27% between August and September, his rate of cash consumption would drop too. Eventually, as the business began to stabilize, a cash surplus would appear – and not before time.

High Note's cash problem is by no means an uncommon one. And there is a cure. Once a business is successfully launched, its sales pattern passes through four distinct stages (see Figure 8.1).

The 'introduction' stage occurs while contacts, customers and a reputation are being built up. Typically, sales and the rate of sales growth are modest and start-up cash resources are adequate.

The next 'early growth' stage is when the problems begin. Rapid sales growth is as natural to a successful new business as physical growth is to a baby. And just as a baby runs out of new clothes, new businesses run out of cash – usually about half-way up the curve.

It is not until the rate of growth has slowed down during the third 'growth' phase that a positive cash flow begins to appear, and much later still before the cumulative net cash flow is in the black.

The fourth stage, 'maturity', is only reached by those who survive the earlier cash flow crisis. This phase is typified by positive cash flow, and a stable sales platform from which to build a strong business.

The key to survival lies in having a good cash-flow forecast, prepared in advance and modified in the light of changing events. This should be used to

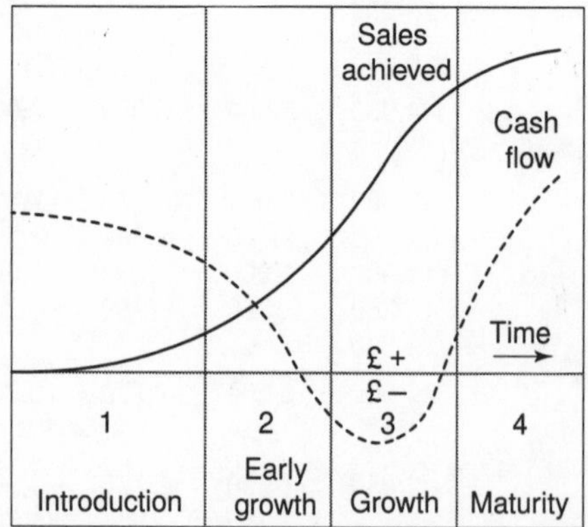

Figure 8.1 Sales and cash cycle for a new business.

negotiate an adequate overdraft facility in advance. But as well as getting help from the bank, small firms can help themselves. The following measures will help you to minimize the need for extra cash to finance sales growth:

- *Send bills out promptly.* Someone new to an area asked his neighbour to recommend a good local builder. His reply was that there was little to choose in workmanship between Brown and Smith, two local firms, but he always used Smith as they settled up once a year!

  Get a system right at the start to get bills, statements and reminders out promptly. Have a hit list of debtors; those who owe money must be chased up for payment. It is a good idea to list debtors by age of the debt as this shows who owes how much and for how long. Take a no-nonsense approach with them and stop supplies to people who take too long to pay or threaten to sue.
- *Check credit ratings.* Before taking on a new or big customer, have them checked out. If they are 'blue-chip' you may be able to factor the debt and get up to 80% of the cash owed immediately. Alternatively, offer discounts for cash and charge interest on overdue accounts. The management of cash flow will produce fewer problems if there are not serious doubts about the likelihood of getting paid.[2]
- *Keep stock levels down.* The chances are that the opening stock will be out of line with customer demand. After all, before the start, companies have to guess what will sell. Once a pattern begins to emerge, order accordingly. Too many new ventures spend all their cash on opening stock, only to find that they are left with products that will not sell and have no cash to buy those that will.
- *Take credit.* As a rule of thumb, successful business people try to take as much credit as they are giving. So if their customers take a month to pay, they aim to take a month's credit from their suppliers.

Understanding the nature of profit

A significant number of new small ventures operate largely on a cash basis. That is, most of their transactions and income come in either as cheques or in folding notes. While it is certainly very pleasant to be able to conduct your business affairs in this way, cash can often give rise to misleading financial signals.

It is very tempting for the owner-manager to believe that the cash that they have in hand is pretty much the same as the profit that they will end up with. And either through feeling flush, or sheer personal necessity, the owner-manager may end up spending more than they can really afford.

The whole problem arises from the difference between the accounting definition of profit, and the 'common-sense' definition of cash. Cash and profits are not the same thing, even in a cash business, and a business needs both cash and profits to survive.

To make matters even more confusing, there are at least three sorts of profit to keep track of! This case history will give you some idea of the problems that can arise.

Example 8.2

Henry Nicholson had worked for a packaging company for five years before it went into liquidation. He had been the area representative for the south-east of London, and had very good contacts with a number of important buyers. His old firm had imported its most profitable lines from Sweden, and when he decided to go into business for himself it was on these that he chose to concentrate.

He took a small warehouse near Southwark Bridge, with an office and telephone. He hired a telephone-sales woman, who chased up orders and 'looked after things' while he was on the road.

The first month's results were quite spectacular, and with nearly £3,000 in his hand Henry Nicholson felt that his future was assured. He had received some £10,000 in sales, and although he still had some of that to deliver, the customers had paid up. They were keen to maintain a source of supply and wanted to do everything they could to help him get started.

He still owed his Swedish suppliers a small amount for one shipment, and he expected that some other bills would come in late in the year. Certainly not every month would be as good as this one and, of course, the taxman would eventually have to be paid. But nothing could alter the fact that he had cash in hand.

Nicholson was a little surprised that neither his bank manager nor his financial adviser was quite as enthusiastic about his trading results (see Table 8.2) as he was. After an hour of probing questions, a new profit and loss account was constructed by his financial adviser (see Table 8.3), with explanations given for the difference between the statements.

Table 8.2 Nicholson's profit and loss account, 1992

	£
Sales receipts	10,000
Less payments for	
Materials	5,000
Wages, etc.	1,000
Rent	500
Advertising	500
Profit for the month	3,000

Table 8.3 Profit and loss account, 1992

	£	£
Sales income		9,000
Less cost of sales		
Opening stock	0	
Purchases in month	6,000	
	6,000	
Less closing stock	500	
		5,500
Gross profit		3,500
Less operating expenses		
Wages, etc.	1,000	
Rent	500	
Advertising	500	
Rates	100	
Telephone	80	
Electricity and gas	80	
Total expenses		2,260
Operating (or trading) profit		1,240
Non-operating expenses		
Loan interest		70
Provision for a personal pension		70
Profit before income tax		1,100
Tax		300
Class II- NI stamps		22
To reserves for future needs		448
Profit available for drawings (net profit)		330

The fundamental differences between cash and profits can best be explained under the following headings.

The realization concept

A particularly prudent sales manager once said that an order was not an order until the customer's cheque had been cleared, they had consumed the product, had not died as a result and, finally, had shown every indication of wanting to buy again. Most of us know quite different salespeople who can 'anticipate' the most unlikely volume of sales. In accounting, income is usually recognized as having been earned when the goods (or services) are despatched and the invoice sent out – not when an order is received, or on the assumption of a firm order, or the expectation of prompt payment.

It is possible that some of the products despatched may be returned at some later date. This means that income, and consequently profit, can be achieved in one period, and have to be removed later on. Obviously, if returns can be estimated accurately, then an adjustment can be made to income at the time.

Nicholson, in our case history, has received a 'pre-payment' for £1,000-worth of goods not yet despatched. This cannot be included in his figure for sales income which has to appear as only £9,000 and not the £10,000 he has received in cash.

The cost of sales

Obviously, goods that have not yet been despatched must still be held in stock. A vital calculation is that of exactly how much stock has been used up over the period. This is calculated by adding the opening stock to any purchases you have made, and taking away the stock that is left. To get this right, you will have to take a physical stock check periodically, but if the volume involved is large, you may have to rely on your paperwork in the meantime.

The 'materials' used in business are usually a major element of expense and as such are separated off from the rest of the expenses. For a manufacturing company, materials are easy to define. For a service business, the sum is less obvious, but still necessary. So, for example, a travel agency's account might look like Table 8.4.

The money that is left after Sunbeam Travel has paid the companies that carry its customers is the gross profit.

Matching expenses

Expenses is the general name given to the costs incurred in selling, marketing, administering, distributing and advertising a company's products or services. Some of these expenses may be for items not yet paid for. The profit and loss account sets out to 'match' income and expenditure to the time period in which they were incurred. In the example above, Nicholson does not have a

Table 8.4 Sunbeam Travel

	£
Sales	200,000
Payment to carriers	130,000
Net commission income (gross profit)	70,000
Expenses, etc. (as for any other business)	

bill for the telephone, electricity or gas, but he cannot enter a nil expense. An estimate of what has been spent is entered. Accountants call this 'accruing'.

A number of other expenses are not allowed for in Nicholson's naive estimate of his profits and once these have been deducted, he is left with £330 to draw as his salary: a far cry from the £3,000 that he originally thinks he has.

Breaking even

While some businesses have difficulty raising start-up capital, paradoxically one of the main reasons that small businesses fail in the early stages is that too much start-up capital is used to buy fixed assets. While some equipment is clearly essential at the start, other purchases could be postponed. This may mean that 'desirable' and labour-saving devices have to be borrowed or hired for a specific period. This is obviously not as nice as having them to hand all the time but if, for example, photocopiers, electronic typewriters, word processors, microcomputers and even delivery vans are brought into the business, they become part of the fixed costs.

The higher the fixed costs plateau, the longer it usually takes to reach break even and then profitability. And time is not usually on the side of the small, new business: it has to become profitable relatively quickly or it will simply run out of money and die. The breakeven analysis is an important tool to be used both in preparing a business plan and in the day-to-day running of a business.

Difficulties usually begin when people become confused by the different characteristics of costs. Some costs, for instance, do not change, however much you sell. If you are running a shop, the rent and the rates are relatively constant figures, quite independent of the volume of sales. On the other hand, the cost of the products sold from the shop is completely dependent on the volume. The more you sell, the more it 'costs' to buy stock. The former of these costs is called 'fixed' and the latter 'variable', and you cannot add them together to arrive at total costs until you have made some assumptions about sales.

Let us take an elementary example of a business's fixed cost: the rent.

In Figure 8.2 the vertical axis shows the value of sales and costs in £000 and the horizontal shows the number of 'units' sold. The second horizontal line represents the fixed costs – those that do not change as volume increases. In this case it is the rent of £10,000. The angled line running from the top of the fixed costs line is the variable cost. In this example we plan to buy in at £3 per unit, so every unit we sell adds that much to our fixed costs.

Only one element is needed to calculate the breakeven point – sales line. That is the line moving up at an angle from the bottom left-hand corner of the chart. We plan to sell out at £5 per unit, so this line is calculated by multiplying the units sold by that price.

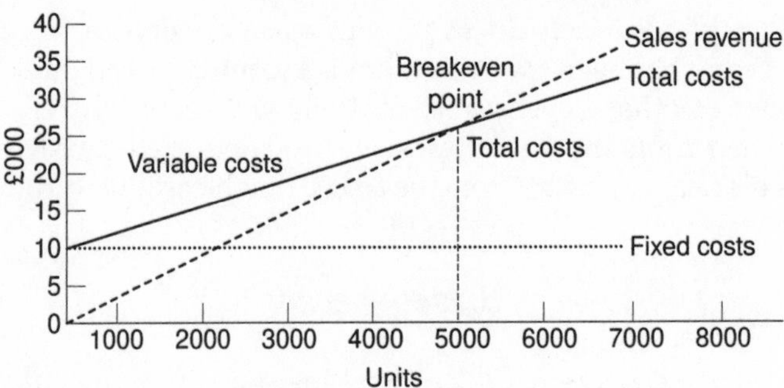

Figure 8.2 Sales and costs.

The breakeven point is the stage when a business starts to make a profit. That is when the sales revenue begins to exceed both the fixed and variable costs. The chart shows our example breakeven point as 5000 units.

A formula, deduced from the chart, will save time for your own calculations:

$$\text{Breakeven point} = \frac{\text{Fixed costs}}{\text{Selling price} - \text{unit variable cost}}$$

$$\frac{10{,}000}{£5 - £3} = 5{,}000 \text{ units}$$

Capital intensive vs. 'lean and mean'

Look at these two hypothetical new small businesses. They are both making and selling identical products at the same price, £10. They plan to sell 10,000 units each in the first year.

Example 8.3

The owner of Company A plans to get fully equipped at the start. His fixed costs will be £40,000, double those of Company B. This is largely because, as well as his own car, he has bought such things as a delivery van, new equipment and a photocopier. Much of this will not be fully used for some time, but will save money now. This extra expenditure will result in a lower unit variable cost than Company B can achieve, a typical capital-intensive result.

Company B's owner, on the other hand, proposes to start up on a shoestring. Only £20,000 will go into fixed costs but, of course, his unit variable cost will be higher, at £4.50. The variable cost is higher because, for example, he has to pay an outside carrier to deliver, while A uses his own van and pays only for petrol.

So the breakeven charts for both companies will be as shown in Figure 8.3 and Figure 8.4. From the data on each company you can see that total costs for 10,000 units are the same, so total possible profits, if 10,000 units are sold, are also the same. The key difference is that Company B starts making profits after 3,636 units have been sold. Company A has to wait until 5,333 units have been sold, and it may not be able to wait that long.

These were only hypothetical cases. But the real world is littered with the corpses of businesses that spend too much too soon. The marketplace dictates the selling price, and your own costs have to fall in line with that for you to have any hope of survival.

Profitable pricing

To complete the breakeven picture we need to add one further dimension – profit. It is a mistake to think that profit is an accident of arithmetic calculated only at the end of the year. It is a specific and quantifiable target that you need at the outset.

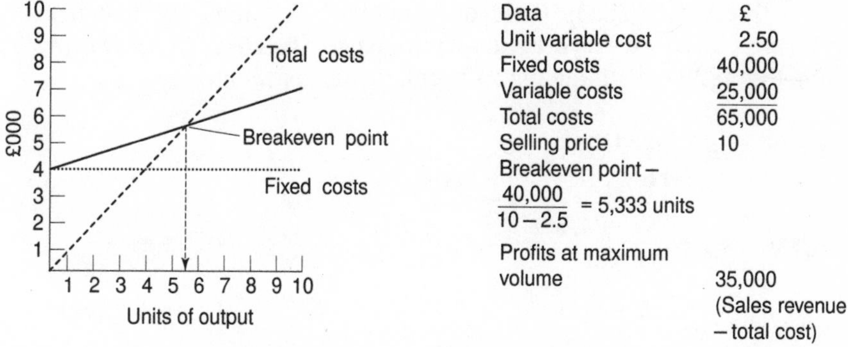

Figure 8.3 Company A: capital intensive.

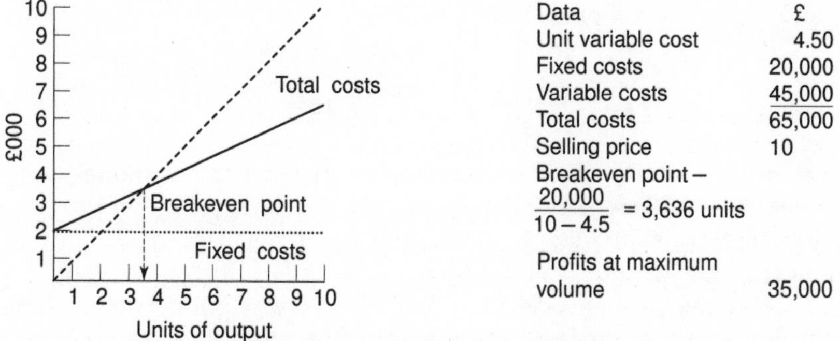

Figure 8.4 Company B: lean and mean.

Let's go back to our previous example. You plan to invest £10,000 in fixed assets in a business and you will need to hold another £5,000 worth of stock too – in all, say £15,000. You could get £1,500 profit just leaving that money in a building society, so you will expect a return of, say £4,000 (equal to 27%) for taking the risks of setting up on your own. Now, let's see when you will break even.

The new equation must include your 'desired' profit so it will look like this:

$$\text{Breakeven profit point (BEPP)} = \frac{\text{Fixed costs + profit objective}}{\text{Selling price – unit variable cost}}$$

$$= \frac{10{,}000 + 4{,}000}{5 - 3} = 7{,}000$$

We now know that, to reach our target, we must sell 7,000 units at £5 each and have no more than £10,000 tied up in fixed costs. The great strength of this equation is that each element can be changed in turn on an experimental basis to arrive at a satisfactory and achievable result. For instance, suppose you decide that it is unlikely that you can sell 7,000 units, but that 6,500 is achievable. What would your selling price have to be to make the same profit? Using the BEPP equation you can calculate the answer as follows:

$$\text{BEPP} = \frac{\text{Fixed costs + profit objective}}{\text{Selling price – unit variable costs}}$$

$$6{,}500 = \frac{10{,}000 + 4{,}000}{6{,}500} = £2.15$$

$$£\times = £2.15 + 3 = £5.15$$

If your market will bear a selling price of £5.15 as opposed to £5, all is well; if it will not then the ball is back in your court. You have to find ways of decreasing the fixed or variable costs, or of selling more, rather than just accepting that a lower profit is inevitable.

From the particular to the general

The example used to illustrate the breakeven profit point model was, of necessity, simple. Few if any businesses sell only one or two products, so a more general equation may be more useful if your business sells hundreds of products as, for example, a real shop does.

In such a business, to calculate your breakeven point you must first establish your gross profit. If you are already trading, this is calculated by deducting the money paid out to suppliers from the money received from the customers. If you are not yet trading, then researching your competitors will give you some indication of the sort of margins you should aim for.

For example, if you are aiming for a 40% gross profit, your fixed costs are £10,000, and your overall profit objective is £4,000, then the sum will be as follows:

$$\text{BEPP} = \frac{10{,}000 + 4{,}000}{0.4^{*}} = \frac{14{,}000}{0.4}$$

$$= £35{,}000$$

(*0.4 = 40%)

So to reach your target you must achieve a £35,000 turnover. You can check this out for yourself: look back to the previous example where the BEPP was 7,000 units, and the selling price was £5 each. Multiplying those figures out gives a turnover of £35,000. The gross profit in that example was two-fifths, or 40% also.

References.

1. Nayak, A. and Greenfield, S., 'The use of management accounting information for managing micro businesses', in A. Hughes and D. J. Storey (eds) *Finance and the Small Firm* (London: Routledge, 1994).
2. Hall, G., *Surviving and Prospering in the Small Firm Sector* (London: Routledge, 1995).

9

Managing the small business

Managing any business is as much an art as a science. Drucker[1] established the five basics of the managerial role: to set objectives; to organize; to motivate and communicate; to measure performance and to develop people. But managing a small business has some unique problems over and above those management problems experienced in larger businesses.

At the heart of many of these problems lie the facts that ownership and management are concentrated in one pair of hands in many small firms, and that rarely in large firms do most people work with or for the person who actually gave birth to the business.

Missions – management starting point

People who have attended management courses recently, or read the heavy-weight business journals like *Harvard Business Review*, will know that one of the current buzz terms is 'mission statement' – and that every business is supposed to have one.

Company chairpersons have taken to quoting their mission statement in the annual report alongside the accounts; founders of new business ventures are expected to print their mission statement up front on their business plan; companies making acquisitions now use their mission statement as an argument to show the logic and synergy behind the bid.

However, a mission statement is not just a trendy gambit for trendy companies; it is a useful tool for a small business to provide a clear sense of direction and thus to ensure that everyone in the company is pulling in the same direction from the outset.

Drawing up a mission statement

A mission statement succinctly sums up what your business sets out to do, and for whom it does it. In the pyramid of goals (see Figure 9.1) the mission statement comes first and the action plans follow later. The end purpose in so many businesses is simply the sum of all the action plans – which is putting the cart before the horse. Remember the saying: 'To the man who does not know where he is going, any road will get him there.' It is the Ansoff[2] cascade, starting with the broad picture and working downwards to specific actions, that is to be adopted in managing a small business effectively.

The mission statement is a statement of direction intended to focus you and your management team's attention on what you do best and for whom you do it. First, the mission should be narrow enough to give direction and guidance to everyone in the business. This concentration is the key to business success because it is only by focusing on specific needs that a small business can differentiate itself from its larger competitors. Nothing kills off a small or young business faster than trying to do too many different things at the outset.

Second, the mission should open up a large enough market to allow the business to grow and realize its potential. One successful small builder defined his mission in the following sentence: 'We will concentrate on domestic house repair and renovation work, and, as well as doing a good job, we will meet customers' two key needs: a quotation that is accurate and starting and completion dates that are met.' When told about this mission, most small builders laugh. They say that it cannot be done. They say that the very nature of the building trade mitigates against being able to concentrate on the specific types of work, or on customer needs. But then many small builders go broke, and the firm laying down the above mission statement is very successful.

Ultimately, there has to be something unique about your business idea,

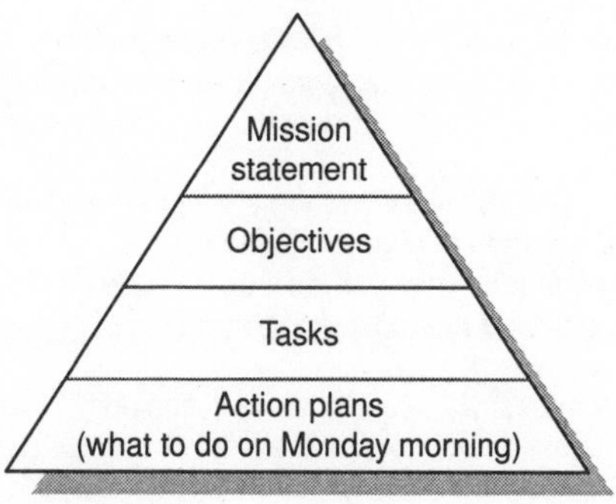

Figure 9.1 The pyramid of goals

yourself, or the way in which you do business, otherwise why should anyone buy from you rather than your competitors? Your mission statement needs to state the essence of that uniqueness.

'Standing by promises' is Tom Farmer's philosophy for Kwik-Fit, and Tom, the son of a Leith shipping clerk, has grown Kwik-Fit into a £150 million-a-year business employing 2,400 people in under two decades. If a Kwik-Fit employee says that he is going to telephone back in half an hour, he does. How many garages do you know that make and keep promises?

In summary, the mission statement should explain what business you are in and it should include some or all of the following:

- ☐ Market/customer needs – who are we satisfying?
- ☐ With what product/service will we meet that need?
- ☐ What are our capabilities, both our particular skills and knowledge and our resources?
- ☐ What market opportunities are there for our product or service and what threats are there from competitors (and others)?
- ☐ What do we enjoy doing most?
- ☐ What do we want to achieve both now and in the future?

Mission statements should be realistic, achievable and brief (no more than a couple of paragraphs).

What mission statements can do for your business

First, they can focus your energy and resources, as the story below illustrates.

Example 9.1

Blooming Marvellous is a company formed by two young mothers in 1980. It started making clothes for children, young mothers and also some general fashion garments. This kept the money rolling in for the first few years, but despite recruiting some good staff, the company failed to grow significantly.

Following a brainstorming session, the founders decided to concentrate their resources on the slice of the market that seemed to offer the greatest potential commensurate with both the company's skills and the founders' personal desires. This led them to produce the following mission statement which provided the focal point for a burst of strong growth:

> Arising out of our experiences, we intend to design, make and market a range of clothes for mothers-to-be that will make them feel that they can still be fashionably dressed. We aim to serve a niche missed out by Mothercare, Marks & Spencer, etc., and so be a significant force in the mail order 'fashion for the mother-to-be' market.

Second, a mission statement can provide a vision for the future.This is the succinct (and informal) mission statement drawn up by bond company, Drexel, Burnham Lambert: 'To be as big as Solomon Brothers so we can be as arrogant as they are and tell them to go and stuff it.'

Drexel, it should be said, has had its problems but it has always had a clear mission statement which told everyone where the business was headed.

A sense of mission

Example 9.2

A manager with a small hosiery firm both impressed and irritated other participants at a training seminar by continually talking enthusiastically about the company he worked for. Although it seemed, in the words of one course member, 'naive, verging on obnoxious', no one questioned the manager's commitment. He clearly identified himself closely with the firm's aspirations. This manager was not suffering from an acute case of business indoctrination – his dedication stemmed from a sense of mission: a rational and emotional belief in his company's products, services and business strategy.

To create a sense of mission within an organization you do need what Andrew Campbell, director of the Ashridge Strategic Management Centre (ASMC), terms 'passionate employees': people who believe that their company is special and are proud of being part of it. 'Many organizations,' claims Campbell, 'have become depersonalized to the point where energy levels are low, cynicism is high and work fails to excite or fulfil employees. We find that committed staff perform many times more efficiently than apathetic ones.'

ASMC's work on the use and misuse of the mission statement concludes that the statements that have most impact on business success are those where a sense of mission exists in the hearts and minds of the employees. Employees not only need a clear understanding of what their company is trying to achieve, but also need to be committed to the company's aims before a meaningful statement can be written. If commitment is lacking, a mission statement is, at best, likely to be ignored and, at worst, treated with cynicism.

ASMC has set out the following five principles to help managers try to create a sense of mission:

- Pick a theme around which to develop the new mission. It should capture the company's future strategy and values and should be easy to translate into behaviours and standards.
- Focus on action rather than words.
- Key standards and behaviours should clearly affirm the company's new direction.

- □ Allow time to develop a mission – it is likely to take weeks and months, not hours and days.
- □ Build and sustain trust. This is often achieved by senior management being visible and open about the changes taking place.

'Leaders should not forget that although a sense of mission is an emotional force, it can be managed,' says Campbell. 'It is an aspect of business which cannot be ignored. An organization with a sense of mission has a strong advantage.'

Do not confuse a mission statement with a slogan: 'Nice people to do business with', 'Traditional service in a modern manner', *et al.* are essentially sales messages and, as such, a vital part of the advertising armoury, but they do not provide a guide to specific action.

Involve as many staff as possible when deciding what your mission statement should be – it is the only way that you will get commitment to the final goals. Show staff other companies' mission statements – tangible evidence that other companies have been through the same exercise will convince them that this is not just the boss's latest whim.

Do not expect to get a perfect mission statement in just a few hours of brainstorming, however. Robert Townsend, who wrote the humorous business classic *Up the Organisation,* claims that it took him six months to capture the essential truth of the Avis business. When he took over the company it was involved in dozens of different businesses from hotels to real estate – and doing badly in most of them. He boiled the mission statement down to this sentence: 'Avis are in the business of renting or leasing vehicles without drivers.' In his own words, he wanted something so clear that the person who drives the elevator could understand and identify with it. You cannot really argue with that.

Finding the people to manage

A Cranfield survey carried out in the winter of 1989 concluded that a fairly staggering 82.7% of owner-managers ranked 'employing key staff' as either their number one or number two business problem, head and shoulders above all the other issues they were worrying about.

Tables 9.1 and 9.2 give some demographic information on the people who responded.

As you can see, just under a third of the survey replies came from those in manufacturing industry, 44.1% from the service sector, 7.1% from wholesaling and 9.5% from the retail sector. Companies were listed as 'other' if their principal activity was given as, for example, exporting or importing, or if they straddled more than one business sector.

Table 9.1 Business sector

Sector	Percentage
Wholesale	7.1
Retail	9.5
Manufacturing	28.7
Service	44.1
Other	10.6
Total	100

Table 9.2 Age of business

Age	Percentage
5 years and under	21.3
6–10 years	29.4
11–20 years	28.0
Over 20 years	21.3
Total	100

Around 50% have been in business for under ten years, and a similar number have been around for a good bit longer (at least one firm responding is 100 years old). So nearly 80% have been through at least one economic cycle – the 1983/4 downturn, the 'boom' to 1988, and the current slowdown. Present economic conditions, therefore, should not be too much of a worry.

Some 47% employ more than 21 people, and about 12% have between 100 and 250 people working for them. But, as you can see from Table 9.3, respondents straddle the whole small business employment spectrum.

Turnover is a relatively crude measure – a service sector company, such as a graphic design studio, would be pretty substantial if its turnover was £0.5 million per annum, while a boat-builder in the same league would be a relative minnow. Table 9.4 shows that half of respondents had a turnover under £1 million per annum, just under a quarter had annual sales of between £1 million and £2 million, and just over a quarter sold more than £2 million. Tables 9.5 and 9.6 show who had plans to grow and the percentage placing each problem in the top two priority positions.

Recruiting key staff

A glance at Table 9.7 will make it clear why employing key staff is such a vital issue to most owner-managers. Nearly 70% of people answering employ people earning £20,000 or more per annum; 44% employ three or more staff at that level and over a sixth have six or more on the payroll. That alone would be enough to make it a problem, but looking ahead to recruitment plans, the situation becomes crystal clear. Nearly 95% planned to recruit one or more

Table 9.3 Number of people employed

Number of people	Percentage
5 people or less	12.0
6–10	13.3
11–20	28.0
21–80	29.4
80 or more	17.3
Total	100

Table 9.4 Turnover level

Turnover	Percentage
Less than £500k	29.3
Between £500k and £1m	21.3
£1m to £2m	21.3
£2m to £5m	13.3
£5m and greater	14.7
Total	100

Table 9.5 Plans to grow

	Percentage
Yes	74.7
No	25.3
Total	100

Table 9.6 Percentage that place each problem in top two priority positions

Problem	Percentage*
Employing key staff	82.7
Finding customers	58.6
Raising new finance	30.7
High interest rates	26.7
Dealing with red tape	21.3

*Total is more than 100%, as multiple problems experienced

Table 9.7 Recruitment plans

Number of staff earning over £20k p.a.	% companies employing now	% number of companies planning to recruit next year
None	30.7	5 3
1–2	25.3	45.3
3–5	26.7	38.7
6–10	5.3	9.3
10+	12.0	1.3
Total	100	100

new key employees next year. A fairly impressive 50% were going to recruit more than three new staff at this salary level, and 10% were looking for even more.

Table 9.8 shows where most owner-managers find key employees. Personal contact is far and away the favoured method, in direct contrast with 'big' business, which seem to favour outside agencies over inside knowledge.

Direct press advertising is the next most popular recruitment method, followed by internal promotion. Right at the bottom of the pile comes the use of recruitment agencies and executive search consultants. These pale into virtual insignificance when compared with the 'do-it-yourself' methods, and a glance at Tables 9.9 and 9.10 shows why.

Table 9.8 How key staff are recruited

Method	Percentage*
Personal contact	49.3
Direct press advertising	37.8
Internal promotion	20.3
File search through a recruitment agency	11.0
Press advertisement through a recruitment agency	9.6
Executive search through a consultancy	9.5

*Total exceeds 100% as people used more than one method of recruitment

Table 9.9 How much spent per key employee recruited

Amount spent	Percentage
Under £1k	59.7
£1,001–£2,000	21.0
£2,001–£5,000	8.7
£5,001–£10,000	6.0
Over £10,000	4.6
Total	100

Table 9.10 How owner-managers felt about the cost of recruiting key employees

Felt the cost was	Percentage
Too low	10.7
About right	73.6
Too high	15.7
Total	100

Over 80% spent £2,000 or less on recruiting the last £20,000+appointee, barely 10% of salary. Nearly 60% spent under £1,000. (It must be said that these figures relate to external expenditure only. At least one proprietor has spent over five weekends and a score of evenings chasing up contacts to find sales staff. If he had costed that time into his recruitment expenditure, his 'bill' would have been several times higher.)

The vast majority, 73.6%, felt that they were paying about the right amount for recruiting staff, with only 10% thinking that they had been a bit mean and 15% a bit generous. This view is in sharp contrast to that taken by 'big business', which would reckon to spend 30%–50% of the first year's salary recruiting staff at this level. A public sector body recently spent more than a year's salary in recruiting someone at a salary of £19,500!

The majority of people surveyed, 59.7%, have made a key appointment in the last two years that has failed. In nearly two-thirds of the cases of a failed appointment, the person stayed in the post for under a year (see Tables 9.11 and 9.12).

It might be that just taking professional advice on recruitment and selection could lower this very high failure rate. The cost per appointment may rise, but if getting the right person first time means that they stay and perform, the overall recruitment costs could fall sharply.

Table 9.11 How many owner-managers made a key staff appointment that has failed in the last two years

	Percentage
Yes	59.7
No	40.3

Table 9.12 How long for key staff in post

Time period	Percentage
Less than 6 months	28.8
6 months to 1 year	37.0
1–2 years	34.7
Total	100

Improving selection

Forty-five seconds, it is claimed, is the time that a typical manager takes between meeting an applicant and deciding whether or not they are the right person for the job. Whether this is true or false, fears that the interview can be a very subjective – and thus biased – way of selecting staff are promoting the trend for companies to use the standard measurement principles when recruiting.

Aptitude and personality tests (called psychometric tests) are among the battery of techniques that are being adapted into industry and commerce from the worlds of educational and clinical psychology. Once the preserve of big companies, the techniques are being used increasingly by small companies to help improve selection for new employees and those in line for promotion, and for self-development by owner-managers themselves.

There are hundreds of different types of tests – not all necessarily reliable (there is no policy body for psychometric testing at present) – which test for different things. If you are considering psychometric tests, make sure that you and the testing organization share the same priorities where aptitudes are concerned.

Job profiling

There are a growing number of psychometric tests that help owner-managers to decide whether a particular person is well suited for the job they are trying to fill. It is reasonably self-evident that being a successful sales person or a successful librarian calls for different sorts of people. They may well be equally intelligent, but their abilities and aptitudes will almost certainly be poles apart.

Fortunately, that is exactly what job profile tests set out to measure. There are usually self-administered, computerized tests, custom designed for the job in question, covering the field from secretaries to sales managers. The tests usually take around an hour to complete, cost upwards of £50, and they can assess both mental aptitude and whether the personality is suitable for the post. The feedback comes in a computer-produced report, which can then be used to help with short-listing.

Team players

Example 9.3

When Mike Arama, chairman of a chain of fifteen petrol stations, was looking for a new accountant, he felt that it was not only vital that the candidate should have good technical skills, but that they should 'fit in' with his existing close-knit team. The psychometric test that Arama chose was the Belbin in conjunction with the Henley Management Centre, which gives individuals a simple means of assessing their best team roles. Dr Belbin's[3] researches led him to identify eight dominant types of team behaviour, as shown in Table 9.13.

Table 9.13 Belbin's team profile

Chairman/team leader Stable, dominant, extrovert Concentrates on objectives Does not originate ideas Focuses people on what they do best	**Company worker** Stable, controlled Practical organizer Can be inflexible but likely to adapt to established systems Not an innovator
Plant Dominant, high IQ, introvert A 'scatterer of seeds', originates ideas Misses out on detail Trustful but easily offended	**Monitor evaluator** High IQ, stable, introvert Measured analyses not innovation Unambitious and lacking enthusiasm Solid, dependable
Resource investigator Stable, dominant, extrovert Sociable Contacts with the outside world Salesperson/diplomat/liaison officer Not an original thinker	**Team worker** Stable, extrovert, low dominance Concerned with individual's needs Builds on others' ideas Cools things down
Shaper Anxious, dominant, extrovert Emotional, impulsive, quick to challenge and respond to challenge Unites ideas, objectives and possibilities Competitive Intolerant of wiliness and vagueness	**Finisher** Anxious, introvert Worries over what will go wrong Permanent sense of urgency Preoccupied with order Concerned with 'following through'

Each type is needed if a team is to be truly effective, and a serious imbalance can cause problems. The Plant (or creator) in Belbin's profile is the kind who is always coming up with new ideas, often radical, and who prefers large-scale planning. The Plant is not, however, remotely interested in implementing their ideas and detailed work bores them. They can be very prickly if criticized and often withdraw into a sulk.

The Company Worker and the Finisher, on the other hand, are practical organizers who can turn ideas into manageable tasks and who are only at ease when they have checked every detail to see that things can be made to work. They have a sense of urgency completely lacking in the Plant.

An organization without a Plant will become sterile and one without Finishers will never get any ideas implemented. Arama uses Belbin to make sure that he keeps a balance in his management team.

Small-business management styles

A Cranfield study into the behaviour of owner-managers and their relationship with key staff in some 200 growing UK companies concluded that owner-managers can be clustered into the following four dominant types of relationship with their staff:

- □ *Heroes.*
- □ *Meddlers.*
- □ *Artisans.*
- □ Or, most desirably, *Strategists.* (Strategists give their managers the tools to do the job and let them get on with running today's business, while they plan for their future.)

The researchers studied two key elements of the relationship between business founders and their organizations. The first element studied was how much time the owner-manager spent on routine management tasks such as marketing, selling, analyzing figures, reviewing budgets or arbitrating between managers. On average, with the exception of the group of entrepreneurs who were still preoccupied with basic non-management functions such as delivering their service or making their product, e.g. architects, small builders, retailers, etc., over 85% of an entrepreneur's working day was spent on these routine management tasks.

The owners' behaviour can be more easily understood by showing this graphically, as set out in Figure 9.2. A low score on the *y* axis indicates either that most time is spent on basic non-management functions, or that most time is spent on strategic issues such as new products for market development, improving market share, acquisitions and divestments, or diversification. A high score indicates that the owner-manager is still largely preoccupied with routine management tasks.

The second element examines what level of business skills has been attained by the key staff and this is plotted on the *x* axis of Figure 9.2. Here a low score would be where most of the management team were relatively new to their tasks or largely untrained for their current job. An example (true, believe it or not) of this would be an unqualified bookkeeper trying to produce the management accounts for a £5 million business. A high score would be where people were mostly either specifically qualified or trained for their current job. If we had replaced the unqualified bookkeeper in our earlier

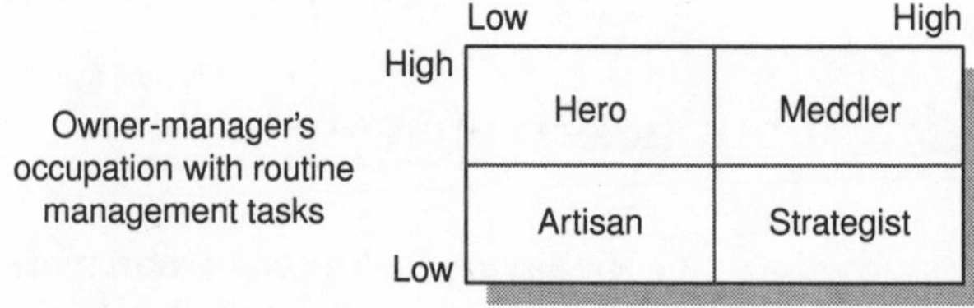

Figure 9.2 Relationship between the owner-manager and their key staff in a growing firm.

example with a fully qualified accountant who had been in post for a year, then this would merit a high score.

The **Artisan** in the Cranfield model is typified by low occupation with routine management tasks – because most of their time is spent producing a product or delivering a service. The level of business skills in the company is also low as most of the Artisan's staff are employed helping in 'production', or carrying out primary tasks such as bookkeeping or selling. The owner-manager is still very much 'one of the boys'. Artisans can encompass professional firms such as architects and surveyors, manufacturers, subcontractors or small building firms, owners of small retail chains such as chemists, video stores and proprietors of hotels and restaurants.

Little time is available either for routine management tasks such as analyzing performance or reviewing models. Every hour that can be sold, is sold, and little time is left over either to improve the quality or profitability of today's business or to consider strategy for tomorrow.

The Artisan has low growth prospects, relative to their market. Their training and development needs are to raise their awareness of the importance of management as a business task of equal importance with daily revenue earning.

The **Hero**, by contrast, probably heads up one management function such as sales or production. But, for example, if they head up sales, they will do little selling except for handling some key accounts. Their time is now spent on managing the business. As the level of business skill of their employees is still relatively low, they will take the lead in initiating routine management procedures. Typically, they will read up or attend a course on ideas such as VAT, accounting, business ratios, market segmentation, sales management and staff appraisal systems. They will introduce these ideas to the firm, and be the only person who really understands them. To their managerially illiterate team the owner-manager will consequently be seen as a hero.

Unfortunately, the Hero has a Herculean task on their hands. Shedding the 'doing' tasks is relatively simple, as working skills in most businesses are either readily available in the local community or people can be trained for them via community training schemes or other job processes, without too much difficulty. But delegating routine management tasks will almost invariably require that the owner-manager first trains their own management teams. There are relatively few well-trained managers available to the small company, for two principal reasons. First, the overall pool of such people is small because training in the small-business sector has, until recently, been almost exclusively concentrated on the entrepreneur. Second, well-trained managers usually seek jobs in larger firms which have more opportunities for advancement and more resources for the practice of the 'art of management'. The Hero has a high capacity for improving the performance of his firm but still has low growth prospects relative to the market. They have no time for strategic thinking and no depth of management to handle growth effectively.

Their training and development needs are to help them raise the general level of management skills in the business, while at the same time increasing their own grasp of motivation, leadership, organization design and development and of strategic management issues in general. If they fail to do this, as most do, they become a meddler.

The **Meddler** raises the level of management skill either by training or recruitment, but then fails to let go of routine management tasks. At this stage, according to the Cranfield model, the owner-manager probably has no functional responsibilities and has assumed the role of managing director. Typically, they spend much time second-guessing, introducing more refined (but largely unnecessary) management systems. They also go on courses or read books that make them even more knowledgeable and sometimes better at routine management tasks than their own subordinates, who anyway are by now doing a perfectly satisfactory job of managing today's business. They get in early and leave late, and practise 'management by walking about'.

One owner-manager in the study still gets in to let the cleaning staff in and leaves at 8.00 p.m. 'when the neighbouring car-park closes'.

The Meddler's problem is that they cannot let go of routine management tasks – because their day will feel empty. They have been used to a seventy- to ninety-hour week, with only ten days' holiday each year. Once their management team is in place and trained, they are out of a job. Until they reduce their involvement with routine management tasks, they will limit the growth capacity of their firm for two reasons. First, the management team will not take on more responsibility if the only reward for taking on the last lot of responsibility was being nagged and criticized. Second, they are too busy checking on people to develop sound strategies for growth.

The **Strategist** is the most desirable type of entrepreneur for the development of a growing business. They develop the management skills of their team to the highest appropriate level and in depth. The Strategist may introduce a staff function to help their line managers in such areas as personnel and market research. This will also free their key managers to think strategically.

The Strategist will devote roughly a third of their time to management tasks such as monitoring performance, coordinating activities, resolving conflict and helping manage today's business.

A further third of their time will be spent motivating, counselling, developing the management team and helping them to manage change. This activity is aimed at improving the existing business. The final third of their time will be spent on developing strategic thinking to form the shape of the future business. Their training needs will be constantly to update their core leadership and motivation skills and to increase their depth of knowledge on strategic issues, acquisition/divestment activity, financing sources and the City.

The natural path of development for the relationship between the owner-manager and their team, is to pass from Artisan to Hero to Meddler and, for the few lucky ones, to become Strategists.

How much management does a small business need?

A small business will need different amounts of leadership and management at different stages in its life and when the environment becomes more (or less) turbulent.

Figure 9.3 is a guide to deciding how much leadership and management is needed at any point in time. The vertical axis shows how much change your company 'needs' at present. This change can either be caused by external factors such as competitors, customers or the economic climate, or it can be self-imposed because the founders may want to change from running a low-growth to a high-growth business. The horizontal axis is the complexity of the business. It can be complex because of its size: for example, the number of products or services offered, or the number of locations in which the business is carried out.

The top left-hand box of the figure is the typical profile for a start-up business. Here, the business is relatively simple, but the change required to create something from nothing is enormous. Leadership is the key skill needed and by definition there is little to manage at this stage.

If the business grows very slowly and stays very simple, doing much the same as when it started, only more so, then it will never need very much leadership or management. The firm will evolve and tick over until it is overcome by a calamity or its profits decline to the point where it would be more profitable to do something else.

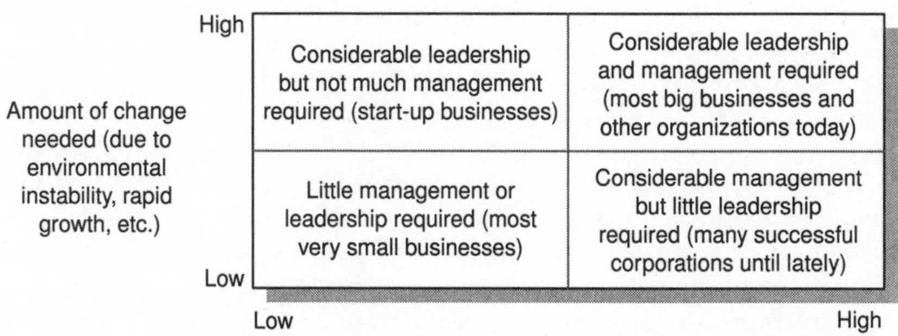

Figure 9.3 The leadership/management matrix.

Example 9.4

Edgar Watts, a firm making willow clefts for cricket bats since 1840, is a good example of this. The company, one of only three in its field, announced its closure in July 1990, making seven staff redundant. Asked why the firm was to close, Toby Watts, 61, the third generation of the family to run the business, said: 'The scarcity of good willows caused by the 1987 hurricane.' But it is hard to believe that this is either the only or the principal reason for the firm's demise. Mr Watts did admit in a subsequent interview that: 'If I was twenty years younger, and prepared to spend five days a week on the road searching for the right trees, we might have been able to save the business.'

However, if after three generations the firm still employed only seven people making the same product in a very stable environment, there was clearly neither the desire for growth nor the need for complexity. The company just had to wait long enough before it was overtaken by events.

More complex businesses that operate in relatively stable environments can usually prosper with lots of management and very little leadership. The problem here is that it is becoming increasingly difficult to locate friendly backwaters that will support a sizeable firm. These firms need to be sure-footed enough to inject sizeable quantities of leadership when the environment becomes unstable, or they too will be swept away.

Example 9.5

ICL up to the early 1980s is a good example of a company that was overmanaged and under-led. Its main customer, the government, was determined that it should stay in business. This created an artificial backwater in the turbulent computer world for ICL, an overcomplex company, to survive in. Mrs Thatcher's attitude to government purchasing threw ICL's management into the competitive arena, where leadership was more important than management. Fortunately, a strong leader emerged and the company just survived.

If you want to achieve rapid growth and, not unnaturally, expect to have to do different things to achieve that growth, your business will need management and leadership in depth. The myth of the solitary hero leader attached to popular entrepreneurs of the last decade has largely been exploded. An army in peacetime needs good leadership at the top and good management below. In wartime it needs competent leadership at all levels.

The business world today is undoubtedly at war and clever companies must learn how to find and recruit people with both leadership and management potential – small firms cannot afford leaders and managers so the skills must often be combined in one person.

Delegation – the key to the owner-manager's survival

Overwork is a common complaint of the small-business owner; too much work and never enough hours in the day to do it. However, it is a problem that could easily be remedied by some effective delegation.

Delegation is the art of getting things done through other people.

Fear of delegation

Most owner-managers are proud of the fact that they have built up their own companies from nothing. In the beginning, entrepreneurs often perform all the tasks of running the business. Reasonable enough, but as the operation grows they may hang on to too many jobs. They may believe that nobody else can do the job, and conversely it is just possible that they may fear being shown up. It is also possible that, through the pressure of work or else the gradual nature of the expansion, they simply have not reviewed the day-to-day management of their time.

Another reason for small-business owners not delegating is that sometimes the routine is preferable to the difficult. Writing invoices is easier than preparing the new cash flow for the bank!

What has to be recognized is that when you delegate, both you and your employees get a chance to broaden their skills. Through delegation you can ease your job of managing and thereby increase the effectiveness of both yourself and your workers – and thus your organization.

The benefits of delegation

- ☐ *Allows time to achieve more.* An owner-manager who can delegate effectively is likely to achieve greater output. Through the proper selection, assignment and coordination of tasks, a manager can mobilize resources to achieve more results than would have been possible without skilful delegation.
- ☐ *Allows time for managerial activities.* Delegation allows the owner-manager an opportunity to handle aspects of the job that no one else can do. For example: project planning, plans for developing the business, monitoring how the business is doing, monitoring staff performance and dealing with any problems arising.
- ☐ *Provides you with back-up.* By delegating responsibility in different areas you will create a back-up workforce who can take over in times of emergency.

Benefits for employees

- □ *Develops employees' skills.* Owner-managers who fail to delegate effectively deprive employees of opportunities to improve their skills and assume greater responsibility. Since employees are likely to realize that they are not learning and gaining experience, they may well leave your firm in order to find a more challenging and supportive environment. This happens most frequently with those employees who are the most talented – precisely the people that you least want to lose. What is a routine job for you is often a growth opportunity for an employee.
- □ *Increases employee involvement.* Proper delegation encourages employees to participate more in understanding and influencing their work. By increasing their involvement in the workplace you will also increase their enthusiasm and initiative for their work.

Benefits for the organization

- □ *Maximizes efficient output.* Making the best use of available human resources achieves the highest possible rate of productivity. Delegation also provides the right environment for employees to offer new ideas that can improve the flow and operation of the workplace.
- □ *Produces faster and more effective decisions.* An organization is most responsive to changes in the environment when individuals closest to the problems are making the decisions about resolving those problems.
- □ *Increases flexibility of operation.* Effective delegation trains several people to perform the same tasks. As a result, when someone is absent or when a crisis requires others to assist with functions not regularly a part of their job, several individuals will already be familiar with the assignment.
- □ *Prepares more people for promotion or the rotation of responsibilities.* It therefore eases your job of finding someone to supervise when you are absent.

A five-point plan

1. *Decide what to delegate and what not to delegate.* The general guidelines that you should follow for deciding what should be delegated include:
   (a) the work can be handled adequately by your workers
   (b) all necessary information for decision-making is available to the worker being delegated the task
   (c) the task involves operational detail rather than planning or organization
   (d) the task does not require skills unique to the owner's position

(e) an individual other than you has or can have direct control over the task.

Therefore any routine jobs, or information collection or assignment involving extensive details such as making calculations, etc., are all things that can be delegated.

Tasks that should not be delegated include the delegation process itself, employee evaluations and discipline, planning and forecasting, confidential tasks, complex situations and sensitive situations.

2. *Decide to whom to delegate.* Obviously your ability to delegate will be governed by the size and quality of your workforce at any given time. However, three factors are of primary importance when selecting the right person for an assignment:

   (a) an employee's skills
   (b) employee interest
   (c) employee workload.

3. *Communicate your decision.* Describe what it is you are delegating and give the other person enough information to carry out the task. Presenting the directive in writing will prevent the 'I don't know' syndrome. If a gap exists between the assignment and an employee's skills, you must be very clear and concise in describing the steps of the task.

   Bear in mind that a new assignment, particularly one involving several stages, is unlikely to be completely understood on the first explanation. Make yourself available for further clarification as the employee works through the assignment. Closely monitoring the employee will save time in the long run.

4. *Manage and evaluate.* From the beginning, clearly establish set times when you will meet the person to review their performance. The secret of delegation is to follow up.

5. *Reward.* Results that are recognized get repeated. You must monitor and respond to the person's performance. Otherwise it is like playing a game without keeping score, which in the end is not motivating.

Part of the essence of delegation is thoughtfully judging when a new employee is ready to handle a more stimulating assignment. If necessary, delegate in stages, starting with small tasks and working up to more challenging projects.

Of course, the one thing that you can never delegate is accountability. No matter which employee handles the task, as the business owner it is your reputation that is on the line.

Delegation is a form of risk-taking – if you cannot deal with a few mistakes, you will never be able to delegate. None the less, effective delegation which is carefully planned and well executed will result in freeing some of your time and also in a more efficient and more profitable business.

References

1. Drucker, P. F., *The Practice of Management* (New York: Harper & Row, 1954).
2. Ansoff, H. I., *Corporate Strategy* (New York: McGraw-Hill, 1965).
3. Belbin, M., *Management Teams: Why They Succeed or Fail* (Oxford: Butterworth Heinemann, 1984).

10

The business plan

One feature that distinguishes small businesses from large ones is an absence of strategic planning in general and of a business plan in particular. The ability to recognize the need for a business plan is now widely regarded as a sign of both business maturity and the likelihood of survival. Nevertheless, developing such a plan is critical to a small firm's survival and success.[1]

From the figures in Table 10.1 it is clear that over the period when small businesses are at their most vulnerable, they have no plan to guide or determine their actions.

One reason that so many small firms are able to start up without a business plan is because founders do not require outside funds or banking support. They either have funds of their own or from a supportive family; or they prefer to pledge personal assets, perhaps by way of mortgage finance, rather than subject their business idea to a potentially harsh review.

Perhaps the most important step in launching any new venture or expanding an existing one is the construction of a business plan. Such a plan must include goals for the enterprise, both short- and long-term; a description of the products or services on offer and the market opportunities anticipated for them; and finally, an explanation of the resources and means to be employed to achieve goals in the face of likely competition.

Table 10.1 Age of firms with a business plan

Age of business	Proportion with current business plan %
0–1 years	25
1–3 years	50
3–5 years	75
5+	95

Source: Cranfield Survey, 1990.

Preparing a comprehensive business plan along these lines takes time and effort. In our experience at Cranfield on our new enterprise programmes, anything between 200 and 400 work-hours are needed, depending on the nature of the business and how much data have already been gathered. Nevertheless, such an effort is essential if small business founders are both to crystallize and focus their ideas, and to test their resolve about entering or expanding their business. Once completed, the business plan will serve as a blueprint to follow which, like any map, improves the user's chances of reaching their destination.

The benefits

There are a number of other important benefits that can be anticipated from preparing a business plan. These include the following:

- Few businesses can grow without additional finance. While it would be an exaggeration to say that a business plan is a passport to sources of finance, without it a business will not really know how much money is needed to finance growth and few organizations will lend or invest in a business without a plan.
- A systematic approach to planning enables mistakes to be made on paper, rather than in the marketplace. One potential entrepreneur made the discovery while gathering data for his business plan that the local competitor he thought was a one-man band was in fact the pilot operation for a proposed national chain of franchised outlets. This had a profound effect on his marketing strategy!

  Another entrepreneur found out that, at the price he proposed charging for a new product, he would never recover his overheads or break even. Indeed, 'overheads' and 'break even' were themselves alien terms before he embarked on preparing a business plan. This naive perspective on costs is by no means unusual.
- A business plan will force the management team to think out their ideas and objectives more thoroughly than they might otherwise,[2] and make them more confident that they can achieve the strategic goals set. They will then be better able to communicate the company's strategy to others in such a way that it will be easier for them to understand and therefore appreciate the reasoning behind the plans.

  This will give both appearance and substance to your having management 'in depth', which is absolutely essential for organizations moving along the continuum from 'one-man band' to major enterprise.
- Preparing a business plan will give you an insight into the planning

process. It is this process itself that is important to the long-term health of a business, and not simply the plan that comes out of it. Businesses are dynamic, as are the commercial and competitive environments in which they operate. No one expects every event as recorded on a business plan to occur as predicted, but the understanding and knowledge created by the process of business planning will prepare the business for any changes that it may face, and so enable it to adjust quickly.

Despite these many valuable benefits, thousands of would-be entrepreneurs still attempt to start without a business plan. The most common among these are businesses that either appear to need little or no capital at the outset, or whose founders have funds of their own; in both cases it is believed unnecessary to expose the project to harsh financial appraisal.

The former hypothesis is usually based on the easily exploded myth that customers will all pay cash on the nail and competitive suppliers are thinner on the ground than optimistic entrepreneurs think. In any event, two important market rules still apply: either the product or service on offer fails to sell like hot cakes and mountains of unpaid stocks build up, all of which eventually have to be financed; or it does sell like hot cakes and more financially robust entrepreneurs are attracted into the market. Without the staying power that adequate financing provides, these new competitors will rapidly kill off the would-be entrepreneur.

Those would-be entrepreneurs with funds of their own, or worse still, borrowed from 'innocent' friends and relatives, tend to think that the time spent in preparing a business plan could be more usefully (and enjoyably) spent looking for premises, buying a new car, or installing a microcomputer. In short, anything that inhibits them from immediate action is viewed as time-wasting.

As most people's initial perception of their business venture is flawed in some important respect, it follows that jumping in at the deep end is risky – and unnecessarily so. Such flaws can often be discovered cheaply and in advance when preparing a business plan; they are always discovered in the marketplace, invariably at a much higher and usually fatal cost.

The ingredients of a business plan

A well-constructed and well-presented business plan needs these five ingredients:

1. Packaging.
2. Layout and content.
3. Writing and editing.

4. Focused recipient.
5. Oral presentation.

Packaging

Every product is enhanced by appropriate packaging and a business plan is no exception. The panellists at Cranfield's enterprise programmes prefer a simple spiral binding with a plastic cover on the front and back. This makes it easy for the reader to move from section to section, and it ensures that the plan will survive frequent handling. Stapled copies and leather bound tomes are viewed as undesirable extremes.

A near letter quality (NLQ) printer will produce a satisfactory type finish which, together with wide margins and double spacing, will result in a pleasing and easy-to-read document.

Layout and content

There is no such thing as a 'universal' business plan format. That being said, experience at Cranfield has taught us that certain layouts and contents have gone down better than others. These are our guidelines to producing an attractive business plan which tries to cover both management requirements and the investor's point of view. Not every subheading will be relevant to every type of business, but the general format can be followed, with emphasis laid as appropriate.

First, the cover should show the name of the company, its address and telephone number and the date on which this version of the plan was prepared. It should confirm that this is the company's latest view on its position and financing needs. If your business plan is to be targeted at specific sources of finance, it is highly likely that you will need to assemble slightly different business plans, highlighting areas of concern to lenders as opposed to investors, for example.

Second, the title page, immediately behind the front cover, should repeat the above information and also give the founder's name, address and telephone number. A home number can be helpful for investors, who often work irregular hours – rather as you probably do. They are likely to be the first point of contact and anyone reading the business plan may want to talk over some aspects of the proposal before arranging a meeting.

The executive summary

Ideally one, but certainly no longer than two pages, the executive summary should follow immediately behind the title page.

Writing up the executive summary is not easy but it is the most important single part of the business plan; it will probably do more to influence whether or not the plan is reviewed in its entirety than anything else you do. It can also make the reader favourably disposed towards a venture at the outset – which is no bad thing.

These two pages must explain the following:

- The current state of the company with respect to product/service readiness for market, trading position and past successes if already running, and key staff on board.
- The products or services to be sold and to whom they will be sold, including details on competitive advantage.
- The reasons that customers need this product or service, together with some indication of market size and growth.
- The company's aims and objectives in both the short and longer term, and an indication of the strategies to be employed in getting there.
- A summary of forecasts, sales, profits and cash flow.
- How much money is needed, and how and when the investor or lender will benefit from providing the funds.

Obviously, the executive summary can only be written after the business plan itself has been completed.

The table of contents

After the executive summary follows a table of contents. This is the map that will guide the new reader through your business proposal and on to the 'inevitable' conclusion that they should put up the funds. If a map is obscure, muddled or even missing, then the chances are that you will end up with lost or irritated readers unable to find their way around your proposal.

Each of the main sections of the business plan should be listed and the pages within that section indicated. There are two valid schools of thought on page numbering. One favours a straightforward sequential numbering of each page, 1, 2, 3 . . . 9, 10, for example. This seems to us to be perfectly adequate for short, simple plans dealing with uncomplicated issues and seeking modest levels of finance.

Most proposals should be numbered by section. In the example that follows, the section headed 'The business and its management' is Section 1, and the pages that follow are listed from 1.1 to 1.8 in the table of contents, so identifying each page as belonging within that specific section. This numbering method also allows you to insert new material without upsetting the entire pagination during preparation. Tables and figures should also be similarly numbered.

Individual paragraph numbering, much in favour with government and civil service departments, is considered something of an overkill in a business plan and is to be discouraged, except perhaps if you are looking for a large amount of government grant.

The table of contents below shows both the layout and content which in our experience is most in favour with financial institutions.

Sample table of contents

Promotional plans
Choice of location and premises
Distribution channels
Anticipated mark-up
Competitor response
Market share projection
Economic, political, social, legal factors that affect strategy
The sales forecast 3.8

4. Selling

Current selling method(s) 4.1
Proposed selling method(s) 4.2
Sales team 4.3
In-house support 4.4

5. Management and staffing

Specific management roles for existing and planned staff and general organization of the business under each 5.1
Strategies for retaining and motivating key staff 5.2
Planned recruitment and selection 5.3
Reward and recognition packages and their relationship to the required business performance 5.4
Appraisal system 5.5
The training and development plan 5.6
A summary of the plan for change 5.7

6. Manufacturing

Make or buy considerations 6.1
The manufacturing process 6.2
Facilities needed 6.3
Equipment and machinery needed 6.4
Output limitation, if any, and scale-up possibilities 6.5
Engineering and design support 6.6
Quality control plans 6.7
Staffing requirements 6.8
Sources of supply of key materials 6.9

7. Acquisition, mergers, joint ventures and divestments

Logic for acquisition 7.1
Target profile 7.2
Plans for search 7.3

8. Forecasts and financial data

Summary of financial performance ratios, ROI, etc.	8.1
Summary sales forecasts	8.2
Assumptions underpinning financial forecasts	8.3
Profit and loss accounts	8.4
Cash flow forecasts	8.5
Balance sheets	8.6
DCF/PAYBACK period for any major investments	8.7
Sensitivity analysis	8.8

9. Financing requirements

Current shareholders, loans outstanding, etc.	9.1
Funds required and timing, including leasing plans	9.2
Use of proceeds	9.3
The deal on offer	9.4
Anticipated gearing and interest cover	9.5
Exit routes for investor	9.6

10. Business controls

Financial	10.1
Sales and marketing	10.2
Manufacturing	10.3
Other controls	10.4

Appendices should include:

Management team biographies

Names and details of professional advisers

Technical data and drawings

Details of patents, copyright, designs

Audited accounts

Consultants' reports or other published data on products, markets, etc.

Orders on hand and enquiry status

Detailed market research methods and findings

Organization charts

Writing and editing

The entrepreneur and their colleagues should write the first draft of the business plan themselves. The niceties of grammar and style can be resolved later. Different people in the team may have been responsible for carrying out the various research needed, and writing up the section(s) of the business plan for which they are most responsible. This information should be circulated to ensure that:

- Everyone is still heading in the same direction.
- Nothing important has been missed out.

A 'prospectus', such as a business plan seeking finance from investors, can have a legal status, turning any claims you may make for sales and profits (for example) into a 'contract'. Your accountant and legal adviser will be able to help you with the appropriate language that can convey your projections without giving them contractual status.

This would also be a good time to talk over the proposal with a 'friendly' banker or venture capital provider. They can give an insider's view as to the strengths and weaknesses of your proposal.

When the first draft has been revised, then comes the task of editing. Here the grammar, spelling and language must be carefully checked to ensure that your business plan is crisp, correct, clear and complete – and not too long. If writing is not your trade, then once again this is an area in which to seek help. Your local college or librarian will know of someone who can produce 'attention capturing' prose, if you yourself do not.

However much help an entrepreneur gets with writing up their business plan, it is still just that – their plan. So the responsibility for the final proofreading before it goes out must rest with them. Spelling mistakes and typing errors can have a disproportionate influence on the way that your business plan is received.

The other purpose of editing is to reduce the business plan to around twenty pages. However complex or sizeable the venture, outsiders will not have time to read it if it is longer – and insiders will only succeed in displaying their muddled thinking to full effect. If your plan includes volumes of data, tables, graphs, etc., then refer to them in the text, but confine them to an appendix.

The text (not the table or appendices) of your final business plan should be eminently readable if you want to stay out of the reject pile in lenders' and investors' offices. The 'Fog Index' can help you make sure that the business plan is readable.

Research into the subject has shown that two things make life hard for readers: long sentences and long words. Back in 1952 Robert Gunning, a business language expert, devised a formula to measure just how tough a letter, report or article is to read.

Called the 'Fog Index', the formula takes the following four simple steps to arrive at a result:

1. Find the average number of words per sentence. Use a sample at least one hundred words long. Divide total number of words by number of sentences. This gives you average sentence length.
2. Count the number of words of three syllables or more per 100 words. Do not count: (a) words that are capitalized; (b) combinations of short easy words – like 'start-up'; (c) verbs that are made up of three syllables by adding 'ed' or 'es' – like 'created' or 'trespasses'.
3. Add the two factors above and multiply by 0.4. This will give you the Fog Index. It corresponds roughly with the number of years of schooling a person would require to read a passage with ease and understanding.
4. Check the results against this scale:

   4 and below, very easy – perhaps childish

   5 or 6, fairly easy – tabloid press, hard-sell letters

   7 or 8, standard – *Daily Mail*, most business letters

   9 to 11, fairly difficult – *The Times*, good product literature

   12–15, difficult – *Economist*, technical literature

   17 or above, very difficult – *New Scientist*, no business use, except to bamboozle.

Focused recipient

Clearly a business plan will be more effective if the writer has a reader in mind.

This will involve some research into the particular interests, foibles and idiosyncrasies of financial institutions. If you are only interested in raising debt capital, the field is narrowed to the clearing banks for the main part. If you are looking for someone to share the risk with you, then you must review the much wider field of venture capital. Here, some institutions will only look at proposals over a certain capital sum, such as £250,000, or will only invest in certain technologies.

It is a good idea to carry out this research before the final editing of your business plan, as you should incorporate something of this knowledge into the way that your business plan is presented. For example, you may find that slightly different versions of section 9.4, 'The deal on offer', have to be made for each different source of finance to which you send your business plan.

Do not be disheartened if the first batch of financiers you contact do not sign you up. One Cranfield enterprise programme participant had to approach twenty-six lending institutions, ten of them different branches of the same organization, before getting the funds she wanted. One important piece of information that she brought back from every interview was the reason for the refusal. This eventually led to a refined proposal that won through.

It is as well to remember that financial institutions are far from infallible, so you may have to widen your audience to other contacts.

Example 10.1

Anita Roddick, the Body Shop founder, was turned down flat by the banks in 1976, and had to raise £4,000 from a local Sussex garage owner. This, together with £4,000 of her own funds, allowed the first shop to open in Brighton. Today there are 100 outlets in the United Kingdom and a further 250 abroad. The company has a full listing on the Stock Exchange, Ms Roddick is a millionaire many times over – and one Sussex bank manager at least must be feeling a little silly!

Finally, how long will it all take? This also depends on whether you are raising debt or equity, the institution you approach and the complexity of the deal on offer. A secured bank loan, for example, can take from a few days to a few weeks to arrange.

Investment from a venture capital house will rarely take less than three months to arrange, and will more usually take six or even up to nine months. Two Cranfield business growth programme participants raised substantial six-figure sums during the 1991 recession and took eleven and thirteen months respectively from first approach to getting the cheques in the bank! Although the deal itself may be struck early on, the lawyers will pore over the detail for weeks. Every exchange of letters can add a fortnight to the wait. The 'due diligence' process in which every detail of your business plan is checked out will also take time – so this will have to be allowed for in your projections.

Oral presentation

If getting someone interested in your business plan is half the battle in raising funds, the other half is the oral presentation. Any organization financing a venture will insist on seeing the team involved presenting and defending their plans – in person. They know that they are backing people every bit as much as the idea. You can be sure that any financier to whom you are presenting will be well prepared. Remember that they see hundreds of proposals every year, and either have or know of investments in many different sectors of the economy. If this is not your first business venture, they may even have taken the trouble to find out something of your past financial history.

Keep the following points in mind when preparing for the presentation of your business plan:

- Be well prepared, with one person (you) orchestrating individual inputs. Nevertheless, you must also come across as a team.
- Use visual aids and rehearse beforehand.
- Explain and, where appropriate, defend your business concept.
- Listen to the comments and criticisms made and acknowledge them politely. You need to appear receptive without implying that you have too many areas of 'ignorance' in your plans.
- Appear business-like, demonstrating your grasp of the competitive market forces at work in your industry, the realistic profits that can be achieved, and the cash required to implement your strategies.
- Demonstrate the product if at all possible – or offer to take the financiers to see it in operation elsewhere. One participant on a Cranfield enterprise programme arranged to have his new product, a computer-controlled camera system for monitoring product quality in engineering processes, on free loan to Fords for the three months when he was looking for money. This not only helped financiers to understand the application of a complex product, but the benefit of seeing it at work in a prestigious major company was incalculable.
- What empathy is there between the financiers and the entrepreneurs? You may not be able to change your personality but you could take a few tips on public speaking. Eye contact, tone of speech, enthusiasm and body language all play their part in making the interview go well, so read up on this – and rehearse the presentation before an audience.

References

1. Scarborough, N. M. and Zimmer, T. W., 'Strategic planning for the small business', *Business*, **2**, 2 (1987), pp. 11–19.
2. Shrader, C. B., Mulford, C. L. and Blackburn, V. L., 'Strategic and operational planning: uncertainty and performance in small firms', *Journal of Small Business Management*, **27**, 4 (1989), pp. 45–60.

11

Exit routes

Every year tens of thousands of small business founders sell up all or part of their business. The reasons for doing so are legion. Some want to retire, others want to get out of a business they are bored with and to use the resources to get into something new. Some feel that their business has reached the point where association with a larger business is desirable or even essential.

Many firms who have taken venture capital on board will find that their erstwhile 'partners' become restive after a few years and seek to influence both the choice and the timing of an 'exit-route' for their investee firms.

These examples give a flavour of some of the main reasons that entrepreneurs give for selling up.

Example 11.1

From its origins in a garage in the early 1970s one small British manufacturer of scientific instruments managed to finance expansion from retained profits. Despite all the efforts of its management, however, the company faced three seemingly insuperable barriers to growth: it lacked the resources to develop its own computer systems; it was unduly dependent on an overseas supplier; and it was unable to break into the US market because its products were not sufficiently competitive. These problems were compounded by a new product which suffered from technical and design failings.

By 1978, the company, which then employed twenty people, appeared to have reached a limit to its growth. It was helped out of this impasse when it was acquired by a larger company. This allowed the smaller firm to finance a new research and development programme and invest in product capacity.

With the help of its larger parent, the smaller company has since grown to a turnover of £11 million (in 1987) and a workforce of 245. Of the company's production 70% is exported and it spends 12% of turnover on R&D.

Example 11.2

In January 1991 Thomas Goode's sixty family shareholders decided that the business, which had been financially weakened in recent years by failed diversifications and the tough retailing market, could best be taken forward as part of a larger organization.

They also wanted to realize some of the capital tied up in the business, which they hoped would fetch about £10 million.

Hambros Bank was asked to look for suitable buyers and very quickly received several preliminary offers from potential purchasers in the United Kingdom as well as from North America, Japan and continental Europe.

The business started in 1827 when Thomas Goode opened a china store in Hanover Square. The shop moved in 1845 to its present site in South Audley Street and consists of an enticing maze of small showrooms displaying ornate glassware, porcelain and fine china.

Mrs Robinson, a former executive editor of *Vogue* magazine who also worked as a main board director at Debenhams, gradually transformed the business after her appointment as managing director in 1988 and also brought in outside professional managers.

The new managers modernized the shop, speeded up service, introduced computer technology, achieved faster stock turn-round and improved the availability of goods. They also introduced a range of branded goods, ranging from pottery to playing cards, and are looking at further licensing and franchising opportunities.

Thomas Goode has retained three royal warrants, which are proudly on display near the entrance. Other precious objects are also on show and two 7-feet-high Minton china elephants stand guard in the window.

However, by 1991 the company had reached an impasse and was finding it hard to expand without further injections of cash. The company was hit badly by the collapse of a pottery manufacturer it ran in Stoke-on-Trent and an unfortunate – and expensive – attempt to stage an exhibition in the United States on the day the Wall Street market crashed in October 1987.

Like many other UK retailers, Thomas Goode suffered from the harsh trading climate in the early 1990s and was further hampered when some large orders from Kuwait and Iraq were cancelled, due to the Gulf War.

Sales in the twelve months to 31 January rose from £3.4 million to £3.6 million but the company still made a small loss at the pre-tax level.

Example 11.3

Finland's largest private company, Nokia, became the world's second biggest manufacturer of cellular telephones after Motorola of America, after paying £34 million for Technophone, a British company set up seven years ago with a share capital of just £3.3 million.

The agreement made Hans Wagner, Technophone's chairman, and Nils Martensson, managing director, millionaires many times over. Together, they held 60% of the share capital.

Mr Martensson remained in charge of Technophone and joined the board of Nokia-Mobira, the cellular telephone arm of Nokia.

The 1991 deal was the fruit of more than twelve months of talks between the companies. It put Nokia in a position to take advantage of the rapid expansion in demand for cellular telephones expected in the wake of agreement on a common European technical standard and fast-rising usage of the equipment worldwide.

Mr Martensson claimed at the time that both companies would benefit from economies of scale as production volumes increased and from shared research and development.

Technophone was set up in Camberley, Surrey, in 1984 and established a reputation for innovative lightweight telephone designs. It has manufacturing plants at Camberley and in Hong Kong, which together employ 500 people, as well as a research and development staff of 150 at Camberley.

Reasons that private company owners sell up

A study at Cranfield published in 1989 by Sue Birley and Paul Westhead, with support from Price Waterhouse and Lloyds Bank, came up with the following statistics on why entrepreneurs sell up (see Table 11.1).

For the 2,000 owners who responded to this part of the research study, 17% indicated a specific strategic reason and 23% either wished to retire or were selling due to ill health. By far the largest majority, however, were either in receivership (28.7%) or administration (23.9%).

Table 11.1 Reasons that private company owners sell up

Reasons for sale	Number	Percentage
(a) Strategic		
For development	41	2.0
Cash for incorporation of business	40	2.0
Lack of funds	5	0.3
Exchange shares for PLC shares	11	0.6
Wishing to diversify		
Seeks acquisition	14	0.7
Strategy/policy misfit	190	9.4
Explore other interests	59	3.0
(b) Personal		
Retirement	397	19.5
Ill health	53	2.7
(c) Ceased to trade		
Receivership	574	28.2
Liquidation	82	4.0
Insolvency	1	0.1
Administration/joint administration	478	23.5
Minimize capital gains	1	0.1
Tax losses/ceased trading	87	4.3

Where are the exits?

The Cranfield study mentioned earlier revealed for the first time the overall pattern in business sales for a five-year period (see Table 11.2). By far the most

Table 11.2 Exit routes for each year, 1983–7

Year	Private advertised sales	Public listing	USM listing	Third Market listing	Mergers listed on the Stock Exchange	Independent acquisitions on the Stock Exchange	Management buy-outs	Receiver independent company management buy-outs	Private/ family retirement/ company management buy-outs
1983	868	79	88	0	68	43	189	6	13
1984	1,168	87	101	0	90	69	209	8	19
1985	1,393	80	98	0	104	94	255	0	53
1986	1,338	136	94	0	132	115	312	2	56
1987	1,522	155	75	35	161	125	335	1	49
Total	6,289	537	456	35	555	446	1,300	17	190

common method used by owners to realize their investment in their business is sale through advertisement.

The option of a listing on the Stock Exchange, whether it be a full listing or a partial listing on the Unlisted Securities Market (USM) or the then Third Market, was a route used by just over 1,000 businesses during the period studied. However, a listing on the Stock Exchange does not automatically imply that the owner(s) or investor(s) have realized the whole of their equity stake in the economy, but that they have merely diluted their ownership. Thus, for example, only 22% of businesses admitted to a full listing sold shares through an offer for sale. This caveat also applies to the 446 independent acquisitions listed on the Stock Exchange.

Over the five years, the results show a clear growth in exit-route activity in all markets except for the USM which has remained fairly stable at around ninety businesses per year. The smaller number in 1987 reflects the October stock market crash of that year. The Third Market was initiated in 1987 as a response to the perceived need for a market in the shares of the smaller, newer business, but in the first year only thirty-five businesses were traded. These positive trends in exit-route activity are also reflected in the growth of management buy-outs, which continue to be an attractive option for entrepreneurs and managers alike. It is too early, as yet, to measure the performance of AIM, the Alternative Investment Market, which has taken over from the USM, as the UK's junior stock market.

Who can help?

Leaving aside going public, Table 11.3 covers the principal organizations involved in selling private companies in the United Kingdom.

Over the five-year period covered in the Cranfield study, 624 agencies were involved in advertising 3,322 private business sales. A significant minority of companies advertised their own firms themselves.

Not surprisingly, the majority of agencies represented the leading firms of chartered accountants, most of which have significant geographic coverage. However, even the twenty most 'active' agencies listed in Table 11.3 accounted for only 27.4% of the advertised sales. Indeed, 537 firms (86.1%) appeared to have very little experience on which to draw, since they were only involved with one or two sales during the five-year period. On the basis of this evidence it was decided in the Cranfield study to classify 'active' agencies as being those agencies that had dealt with more than ten private sales each over the five-year period.

The media used by these organizations to sell private companies were studied in a two-month sample out of the whole period. To do anything else would have involved an enormous volume of data and perhaps hide greater

Table 11.3 The leading agencies advertising private sales, 1983–7

Agency	Number of business sales	% of total business sales
Peat Marwick McLintock	284	4.5
Grant Thornton	204	3.2
Cork Gully	155	2.5
Price Waterhouse	117	1.9
Arthur Anderson	111	1.8
Touche Ross	108	1.7
Arthur Young	94	1.5
Ernst & Whinney	93	1.5
Deloitte, Haskins & Sells	83	1.3
Spicer, Pegler & Partners	67	1.1
Robson Rhodes	59	0.9
Stoy Hayward	55	0.9
Edward Symmons & Partners[a]	46	0.7
Henry Butcher Business Brokerage[a]	46	0.7
Binder Hamlyn	37	0.6
Coopers & Lybrand	37	0.6
Humberts Chartered Surveyors[a]	37	0.6
Christie & Co[a]	35	0.6
A. P. Locke & D. R. F. Sapte	32	0.5
Levy Gee & Partners[a]	26	0.4

Note: [a] Essentially dealing in real estate

accuracy. Alongside the heavyweight nationals, the specialist periodical *Business and Assets* and a representative local newspaper, the *Western Mail*, were included.

Table 11.4 shows that the *Financial Times, Daily Telegraph* and the *Western Mail* were all important media for the sale of private companies.

The *Financial Times* was particularly strong with regard to manufacturing companies, while the *Daily Telegraph* heads the lists for service companies.

When it comes to the size of businesses being sold, the *Financial Times* is the clear leader (see Table 11.5). The average business on offer was at a price of £455,027 compared with the *Western Mail* where the asking price was only £68,253.

Table 11.4 Industrial category of private business sales by different data sources

Standard Industrial category	Data source									
	Financial Times		*Daily Telegraph*		*The Times*		*Business & Assets*		*Western Mail*	
	No.	%	No.	%	No.	%	No.	%	No.	%
Primary	12	3.9	1	0.4	1	1.5	2	3.4	24	8.7
Manufacturing	112	36.0	7	2.5	13	19.7	26	44.8	7	2.5
Construction	13	4.2	5	1.8	1	1.5	0	0.0	3	1.1
Services	168	54.0	270	95.4	49	74.2	30	51.7	241	87.6
Not known	6	1.9	0	0.0	2	3.0	0	0.0	0	0.0

Table 11.5 Selling price (£s) of private business sales by different data sources, June–November 1987

Data sources	Selling price (£s)					
	Mean	Standard deviation	Minimum	Maximum	No. of valid cases	% of valid cases
Financial Times	455,027	526,780	3,500	3,000,000	55	17.7
Daily Telegraph	288,988	284,692	20,000	2,000,000	225	79.5
The Times	174,513	208,048	10,500	1,100,000	36	54.5
Business & Assets	230,667	164,020	50,000	450,000	6	10.3
Western Mail	68,253	70,957	1,875	600,000	172	62.5

Preparing for the sale

For the small-business founder thinking of selling it certainly pays to plan ahead and prepare the business to look its best. Buyers will be looking, at least, at the last three years' performance, and it is important that figures for these periods are as good and clean as possible.

Taking the latter point first, private businesses do tend to run expenses through the business that might be frowned upon under different ownership. One firm, for example, had its sale delayed for three years while the chairman's yacht was worked out of 'work in progress'. There can also be problems when personal assets are tucked away in the company, or where staff have been paid rather informally, free of tax. The liability rests with the company, and if the practice has continued for many years, the financial picture can look quite messy.

The years before selling up can be used to good effect by improving the performance of the business relative to others in the industry. If the business is firmly planted on an upward trend, future projections will look that much more plausible to a potential buyer. Founders should certainly have a business plan and strategic projections for at least five years. This will underpin the strength of negotiations by demonstrating management skills in putting together the plan, and will show that the management believe that the company has a healthy future.

Some small businesses may wonder if such an effort is worthwhile. Perhaps the following example will show how financial planning can lead to capital appreciation for the founder.

Example 11.4

A 34-year-old owner-manager built up a regional service business in the United States that had a 40% compounded annual growth rate for the five most recent years. He employed an experienced CPA (chartered accountant) as his chief financial officer. This person developed budgets for one- and two-year periods and a detailed business plan charting the company's growth over the next five years. The owner's objective stated to his directors was to be ready to sell his business when the right offer came along.

A UK company interested in acquiring a leading service company in the region and finding a manager with the potential for national leadership carefully analyzed the company and came away impressed with management's dedication to running its business in a highly professional manner. Because the previous year's after-tax profits had been $500,000 on sales of $10 million, the UK company offered $4.5 million on purchase, and $4.5 million on attainment of certain profit objectives (well within the growth trend). The transaction closed on these terms.

The $9 million offering price, representing eighteen times net earnings, was 50% higher than the industry norm and clearly justified the owner's careful job of packaging his business for sale.

A guide to further reading

Arthur, Michael B. and Jones, Alan, *Strategy Through People* (London: International Thomson Business Press, 1995).

Barrow, Colin, *Financial Management for Small Business* (London: Kogan Page, 1995).

Barrow, Colin, *The Complete Small Business Guide* (London: BBC Publications, 1995).

Barrow, Colin and Paul, and Brown, Robert, *The Business Plan Workbook*, 2nd edn (London: Kogan Page, 1992).

Barrow, Colin and Golzen, Godfrey, *Taking Up a Franchise*, 12th edn (London: Kogan Page, 1997).

Coneston, Thomas, *Creating Excellence in Boardrooms* (Maidenhead: McGraw-Hill, 1993).

Crimp, Margaret, *The Market Research Process*, 3rd edn (Hemel Hempstead: Prentice Hall, 1995).

Faulkner, D., 'Measuring product advantage using competitive benchmarking and customer perception', *Long-Range Planning*, **27**, 1 (1994), pp. 119–32.

Fisher, Martin, *Performance Appraisals* (London: Kogan Page, 1996).

Golzen, Godfrey, *Working for Yourself* (London: Kogan Page, 1997).

Gumbert, David E. (ed.), *Growing Concerns: Building and Managing Small Firms* (New York: John Wiley & Sons, 1984).

Hawkins, Barrie and Badge, Grant, *Thinking Up a Business* (USA: Rosters, 1990).

Hayes, Nick, *Successful Team Management* (London: International Thomson Business Press, 1996).

Institute of Directors, *A Guide to Financing Growth* (London, 1995).

Kao, John, *Entrepreneurship, Creativity and Organization* (Hemel Hempstead: Prentice Hall, 1989).

McDonald, Malcolm, *Developing the Marketing Plan: The Marketing Book* (Oxford: Butterworth Heinemann, 1994).

Nash, Tom (ed.), *Buying and Selling Private Companies* (London: Institute of Directors, 1994).

Peters, Thomas and Waterman, Robert, *In Search of Excellence* (New York: Harper & Row, 1982).

Porter, Michael E., *Competitive Strategy* (New York: Collier Macmillan, 1981).

Reay, David G., *Planning a Training Strategy* (London: Kogan Page, 1994).
Richardson, Pat and Clarke, Lawrence, *Business Start-up for Professional Managers* (London: Kogan Page, 1993).
Rosthorn, J., Haldane, A., Blackwell, E. and Whaley, J., *The Small Business Action Kit*, 4th edn (London: Kogan Page, 1994).
Stolze, William J., *Start-up* (Rochester, NY: Rock Beach Press, 1990).
Storey, M. John, *Inside America's Fastest Growing Companies* (John Wilson & Sons, 1989).
Taffinder, Paul, *The New Leaders' Styles and Strategies for Success* (London: Kogan Page, 1995).
Walker, Ian, *Buying a Company in Trouble* (London: Kogan Page, 1992).
Warnes, Brian *The Ghenghis Khan Guide to Business Survival* (London: Osmosis, 1984).
Zairi, M., *Effective Benchmarking* (London: Chapman & Hall, 1996).

Index

Note: Page numbers in *italics* indicate figures and tables; page numbers in **bold** type indicate examples.